BENEATH THE ARMOR OF AN ATHLETE

OF AN ATHLETE

Real Strength on the Wrestling Mat

Lisa Whitsett

Wish Publishing
Terre Haute, Indiana
www.wishpublishing.com

LCCN: 2002109847

Edited by Natalie Chambers
Proofread by Ken Samelson
Cover designed by Phil Velikan
Cover photography by Shannon Tennyson, Tennyson Photography

Printed in the United States of America
10 9 8 7 6 5 4 3 2 1

Published in the United States by
Wish Publishing
P.O. Box 10337
Terre Haute, IN 47801, USA
www.wishpublishing.com

Distributed in the United States by
Cardinal Publishers Group
7301 Georgetown Road, Suite 118
Indianapolis, Indiana 46268
www.cardinalpub.com

Disclaimer: This book is written as nonfiction work and recounts primarily true events. When appropriate and/or for effect, conversations and incidents have been dramatized or created to supplement the story. Likewise, some events have been omitted and some names have been changed at the author's discretion.

For my husband, Steve, who teaches me unselfishness.
For my mother, Doni, who teaches me compassion.
For my father, David, who teaches me strength.
For my grandfather, Herbert, who teaches me wisdom.
For my grandmother, Mary, who teaches me laughter.
For my brother, Eric, who teaches me forgiveness.
For my twin sister, Laurel, the light at the end of the tunnel.

Acknowledgments

The experiences documented in this book would not have been possible without the positive influence of many people. Those people include: Cory Baze; Don and Diana Briggs; Coach Mike Carter; Colorado high schools' wrestlers and parents; the community members of Cedar Falls, Iowa; Dan Gable; Scott Glenn; Sergio Gonzalez; Coach Tadaki Hatta; Sharon Huddleston; Coach Mike Marsh; Coach Roye Oliver; Coach Myron Roderick; Tricia Saunders; Coach John Smith; 1991 Roderick-Smith's camp staff and wrestlers; Doug Stanford and family; Coach John Talbott; 1993 women's winter tour wrestlers; 1989-1994 women's freestyle wrestling teams; University of Northern Iowa wrestlers and coaches; and USA Wrestling.

I wish to thank Holly Kondras of Wish Publishing for her support and patience, and Kathy Sparrow of Blue Mantle Publishing for her encouragement.

Preface

Several years ago, I would have viewed the future only in terms of my sport: freestyle wrestling. I would have shared my detailed plans to obtain a national championship with those who asked, and when I did, I would not have mentioned any other goals, because I did not have any. My sole ambition in life was to be the best wrestler I could be.

Fundamentally, I believe that's okay. Anyone who has ever chased a challenge knows that unwavering commitment is vital to the process. But while my commitment to wrestling focused me on one level, I allowed it to misguide me on other levels. My commitment often cost my physical health, my better judgment, and sometimes, even my morals. I became reckless in pursuit of achievement.

Year after year, though, I minimized the consequences of my behavior, not the least of which included selfishness and difficulty maintaining relationships. Instead, I stayed focused on wrestling. In particular, I stayed focused on conquering the intense competition anxiety that plagued me. It wasn't until later that I made the connection between the anxiety and the issues I had avoided all along: I really had very little idea who I was underneath it all, who I really wanted to be, and I lacked confidence. I was tough on the outside but often vulnerable on the inside. Finally, after a wrestling tournament one day, I was hit broadside with my own denial – I had no idea why I was participating in sports anymore.

If I ever wanted to see a wrestling mat again, I knew I had to address some difficult issues, including redefining myself and rediscovering some lost confidence. It was often uncomfortable, but it was necessary, and eventually I returned to sports for the right reasons. I hope this book encourages you, or another athlete you care about, to do the same.

1

April 1991
Las Vegas, Nevada
National Freestyle Wrestling Tournament

An hour remains. I am four pounds over my wrestling weight. Running the same route I have since early this morning, I pass the drinking fountains and vending machines displaying pictures of life-sized cans of cola. Even that cannot produce enough saliva to coat my tongue, white from dehydration.

The Las Vegas Convention Center is a vast arena, the perfect setting for the men's and women's National Freestyle Wrestling tournament. The venue whirls with the energy of hundreds of wrestlers, including me, pursuing national championships. Nearly every state in the nation is well represented, and Iowa is no exception. I am just one of several, though my counterparts are male.

The arena features endless hallways of blue and fuchsia carpeted corridors, though none were probably ever intended to be weight-cutting pathways for wrestlers. Nevertheless, we have used them each year for that purpose, striving to drop the last pound or two through perspiration. The colors of the floor provide a welcomed distraction while I suck the last drops of precious water from my muscles in an effort to make weight. It is a slow death.

I run for the scale in the weight room. The sudden stopping cramps my calves and gut, but I ignore it and jump on the scale. The numbers bounce back and forth, and finally settle on 104 pounds. I am still over weight at 103.5, by one half of a pound.

My body is not surrendering the remainder of its water and the sauna is my only choice. I draw my hood over my head and yank on the heavy wooden door. It reveals a coffin of a steam room with wide planked cedar boards and a low ceiling. It also shelters a pack of male wrestlers, many of whom are naked trying to drop pounds. None recognize I am female with my hood up.

Blistering heat slaps my face and scorching dry air engulfs me. Every taste bud on my tongue scrapes the roof of my mouth as I wipe the white crust from my full lips, dry like dehydrated fruit, cracked and bleeding. As I hop up and down, squat jump, do anything to perspire, my muscles feel like they're scraping against each other inside my skin. My long locks of brown hair, originally fastened in a ponytail, are loose now, matted by layers of dried sweat, and cling to my gaunt face. My skin, ordinarily light olive is tainted by today's torture and has been replaced with a chalky undertone.

One by one, the other wrestlers exit the sauna for their weigh-in, leaving me alone to bake. The heat seeps through me like hot lead as I touch a weak hand to my face. Sweat is finally beading on my forehead. I rest my head on the back wall and struggle to keep my legs moving. My insides swirl around in the heat and my body eats away at itself. My heartbeat, arrhythmic, pounds out the words in my mind. *I can do this. This pain is expected. Just keep going. I can do this. Whatever it takes.* My lungs constrict and my breathing is shallow. I glance at the clock through the tiny square window in the sauna door. Time has nearly run out. I wipe a tear from my eye with my sweatshirt and emerge from the sauna with the desperate hope I have lost enough water weight.

Only two other female wrestlers and two officials with clipboards remain. They turn to me when I burst from the steaming room. I have two minutes to make weight. I strip to my underwear and step on the scale: 103.6 pounds. My long hair is damp with sweat; I seize an opportunity, however unrealistic and misguided. I beg one of the wrestlers to find scissors to cut it off and she races out of the room on her mission. In the meantime, the other wrestler suggests I try her method: headstands. I approach the nearest wall and flip upside down.

"Lisa, you've got one minute," the official warns, "and then I have to weigh you. No exceptions."

2

I gasp in acknowledgement and more blood rushes to my head. The wrestler has not returned with the scissors and my sweaty hair lays limp on the cement around my head. Time runs out.

"Young lady, get on this scale." The official is firm and out of patience. "Now."

I push off the wall, faint and nauseous as I return upright again. The official helps me regain my balance. I let out a deep breath and step on the scale. The digital numbers bounce back and forth, taunting me. I close my eyes. *Please make this.*

"One hundred three point five pounds," the official announces at last. I open my eyes and lunge off the scale to the water cooler. My hands quiver as I grab for a paper cup and tap the spout. With the cup half full I collapse, still nearly naked, and gulp the water. Most of it runs off the side of my lips. My tongue sticks to the inside of my mouth. I clutch the end of the table to pull myself up and rip open the top of the cooler. I dunk cups into it, fill them with water and gulp, dunk again, continue gulping. I am exhausted, my body a limp piece of strained muscle, and my tongue still feels like sandpaper.

At the tournament the next day, Tricia Saunders' fan section cheers as she steps out onto the mat to wrestle me. My head pounds at the sight of her. Adrenaline pours into my veins. Stone-faced and serious, Tricia is a wolf, hunting her second national championship. My empty stomach rumbles reminding me how nervous I am to wrestle her, so much so I have not been able to eat since before weight-cutting 12 hours ago. I place a hand on my abdomen to silence the growling and feel my fingers, cold as Popsicles even through my singlet. I chew on the inside of my bottom lip, usually healthy pink, now steel blue. Circles beneath my eyes are a matching shade and my nose is ice tipped. My stomach roars again and tenseness swells. I drown in the anxiety. My mind is unfocused and disconnected from the moment, even when the referee blows the whistle to start the match.

Tricia pummels me like a punching bag and a thick shoulder plunges into my gut. Fleeting moments of my aggressiveness, my forehead burrowing into her temple, our foreheads smashing skull against skull, do not begin to ruin her. After only two minutes of wrestling, defeat closes in on me like barracuda. The referee slams his hand to the mat and blows his whistle—Tricia has pinned me. As quickly as the referee raises Tricia's wrist in victory, I rush away to escape the mat.

I dash into a vacant restroom down a deserted hallway, ripping my wrestling shoes off and hurling them by their shoelaces at the cement wall. The subsequent cursing is unbecoming, but it parallels the indignity of the moment. I want to scream, but instead, manage to splash crisp, cool water from a running faucet on my perspiring forehead and brace my arms against the porcelain basin. I stare at my face in the mirror as water droplets trickle off my skin. My blue eyes are worn; the fire behind them extinguished from weight cutting and excessive training. Images of my match barrage the caverns of my mind as I try to neutralize the self-deprecation. Part of me considers that I am inexperienced and still learning, but I know the truth is that I simply fell apart before I even got out on the mat. After significant self-interrogation, I glance at my belongings, strewn about randomly following my tantrum, and gather them from the floor to make my way back out to the arena.

The floor is bustling with wrestlers and their fans, and I find an available place to sit in the Athletes Only section beneath the first row. I roost to watch the rest of the wrestling matches. Amidst the cheers and screams, a young boy's voice resonates from the stands above me. He dangles his frail body as far as he can over the security rail and presents me with a wrestling shoe and a T-shirt.

"Will you sign these for me?" In his other hand, he grips a pen. I scan his face for sincerity as he clings to the rail awaiting my response.

"Are you having fun watching the matches?" I ask as I approach him and take the pen.

"Yeah," he says with a grin. "Did you win?"

I stare up at his expectant face, wishing I could say yes. I cannot, and the painful truth trickles from my mouth. "Not today, I'm afraid. I lost to Tricia Saunders." I sign the shoe with my most careful handwriting.

"She's really good. I have her autograph, too," he says. "Why did you lose to her?"

He means nothing by it, I remind myself. "Because she wrestled better than I did today."

"Have you ever wrestled her before?"

I nod my head slowly in attempts to be patient with his questions. "Lots of times."

"Did you ever beat her?"

"Not yet." I try to change the subject by holding the items up for his inspection. "How does that look?"

The child scrunches his face. "Are you ever gonna beat her?"

I take a deep breath and exhale. "Not if I keep wrestling like I did today, I won't." The truth of it stings me.

He inspects the signed shoe and T-shirt. "Thanks for the autograph," he says. "I hope you win next time." He turns to trot up the bleachers.

"Thanks," I shout after him, but he is already gone. I drop into a folding chair nearby and stare at the mats. As a rule, I keep thoughts of my failures bottled up and locked away, but the little boy's words released them. I shudder as they flood my mind. Frame by frame, I recall Tricia beating me into submission. More to the point, I see myself allowing it. I pull my hood up around my head as the chill from drying sweat settles into my bones.

2

April 1991
Cedar Falls, Iowa

It is a characteristic spring day in my hometown in Iowa: 65 degrees with a light breeze carrying the faint odor of the cattle farms not far away. Soon the high school kids will be working the summer in the cornfields but for now College Hill, the local food and bar area, bustles with the energy of 13,000 college students at UNI, the University of Northern Iowa.

I live on one floor rented in a three-story house that faces the main street on campus. Inside the space, worn but sturdy hardwood planks cover the living room, bedroom, and small kitchen. Double-paned windows are draped in white blinds that fall just to the sills and the textured walls could use a fresh coat of white paint. Wrestling posters, newsletters, and magazines paint the walls and common areas. Piles of sweaty workout clothes await washing and unmatched wrestling shoes lie about the carpet in the bedroom.

I lay belly down on a living room rug with the phone in one hand and a pencil in the other. Glimpses of Tricia beating me flash in my mind. I whimper recalling how nervous I was and how poorly I had wrestled. I pull a pamphlet describing the details of a wrestling camp from my bag, not yet unpacked from the national tournament three days prior. I review the glossy brochure several times before I pick up the phone to dial the contact number listed. I clear my throat and muster confidence. The phone rings once, then twice.

"Wrestling office," the voice announces.

I hop to my feet and request to speak to the head coach.

"Speakin'," the voice says in a Southern twang.

The wood-planked floor creaks while I pace as I share my request to attend the coach's camp. I imagine the coach on the other end, perhaps a man whose values are cemented firmly in societal tradition. I continue pacing.

"The boys let you train with them?"

His tone is judgmental. I toss the brochure back into my bag. Clutching the thoughts of hard work, the training, and my dreams of success close to my heart, I ignore the comment and respond, but not without a lump forming in my throat first. "Sir, my goal is to make the USA women's national team. I really need some more training, so I'd appreciate your serious consideration."

He hardly allows me to finish my sentence. "We've never had a girl at camp before."

"I understand that." I clear my throat. "I would like to attend anyway."

"There's really no place to house you."

"Can't I just stay where everyone else stays? In the dorms or something?"

He scoffs. This request apparently confirms his beliefs. "Alright, come on now, young lady. Be honest. What's your relationship to these wrestlers?"

"What do you mean, 'my relationship to the wrestlers'? I'm a wrestler. That's my relationship."

"USA wrestling didn't say anything to me about any girls wrasslin'. I'm sorry, honey. Gonna have to pass on this."

His dismissal aches in every bone of my body and his insinuations nauseate me. I had become used to maneuvering through the good old boys in the wrestling culture. It was fairly easy to recognize them: generally disapproving toward female wrestling, touting our participation to be an annoyance, an interference to be reconciled. I had bit my lip through several one-sided conversations in which a wrestling fan informed me that women just weren't supposed to do stuff like that, and I learned to pick my battles while ignoring others. Today, for some reason, the discrimination in his tone clutches my heart a little bit tighter than usual. I stew in the coach's dismissal for another moment and finally throw a calculated swing.

"So, your camp is a USA wrestling sanctioned camp?"

"Of course," he acknowledges.

"Then by the rules that govern those camps, you cannot exclude me from it. More importantly, your university's reputation is tied to this camp. I'm certain with the investigations your university has endured this year due to your alleged illegal recruiting practices, you probably don't need anymore negative attention than you have already." I tap a pencil against the arm of the couch while the phone buzzes in my ear. A generation passes before he speaks.

"You know Charlie Henry?" he asks, with what sounds like gritted teeth.

"Yes, sir."

"He's got a camp in two weeks in Greenwood, Colorado. It's a commuter camp—the wrestlers don't stay on a campus— probably be better for everyone." He hangs up. I hold the dead phone in my hand.

It was a lot better than nothing.

I awake from a catnap to a knock at my door.

"Who is it?" I yell from the couch.

"It's your Dad," a melodious voice shouts from beyond the door. "Any hungry wrestlers in there want to go to lunch?"

I lurch off the couch and skip to the door. "I do, I do!" I thrust open the door to find my father awaiting me.

"Hey, Partner." He wraps ample arms around my back.

"Hi, Daddy." I bury my face in his chest. I smell his familiar scent on his favorite hunter green sweatshirt and melt in the comfort of his embrace. I had always felt reassured by him. My twin sister, Laurel, and I moved in with him when we were eight years old after my mom had relinquished custody of us soon after their divorce. In a selfless act of love, my mother decided Iowa would be a much better place for her children to grow up compared to the big city of Los Angeles where she lived.

My father is a psychologist, teaches the subject at the University of Northern Iowa, serves as the college wrestling team's psychologist, and independently consults with businesses. For the latter, he used to travel a lot, but he was rarely out of town for much more than a few days at a time, especially when we were young.

Regardless of the number of days he was gone, though, I longed for him until he would return from the airport and from the brutal Iowa winter, snowflakes on his shoulders, and his corporate suit nearly frozen. Standing on the staircase for height, I would hug him, my cheek to his shoulders. I breathed in with relief. His tie wasn't even loosened yet and I would run to get my homework from school to show him.

He would set his briefcase on the table and sit with me, admiring the work I'd done.

"Looks like you worked hard on this," he would say, studying it. Then he would beam a smile of naturally straight teeth through a mustache and bearded mouth. The wire-rimmed spectacles completed the stereotypical psychologist face. I would nod and shine in his approval. When my dad was proud of me, everything seemed possible.

Now he follows me into the living room and sits in the only chair not occupied by dirty clothes or wrestling gear.

"Glad to be home from Nationals," I continue the conversation. "That was a beating."

"Uh-oh. That doesn't sound so good. Didn't go the way you wanted, huh?"

I roll my eyes and kiss him on the cheek before excusing myself to the other room to dress.

"I don't know what happened." I shout from my room as I race around trying to find clean clothes. "Tricia was rock solid as usual. I couldn't get in on her. She pinned me in two minutes." I omit the part about my nervousness and my inability to focus but it does not distance me from the regret.

"That doesn't sound too fun," he suggests.

I hadn't thought about it that way. "You're right. It wasn't." I find blue jeans and a gray sweatshirt in the back of my closet. I tear through a drawer of athletic socks looking for two that match.

"Did you do your best, though?"

I consider his question. "The best I could do that day," I say, knowing what I'm hiding.

"That's all you can ask for then, isn't it, Partner?"

I appear from the bedroom, fully dressed. "I guess so." I grab my wallet. "How about I pay this time?"

He rises out of the chair and then feigns stumbling backwards. "What? My daughter is paying for lunch? Be still my heart."

I laugh. "Hey, I could change my mind, you know."

"You've been known to do that before." He smiles. "Okay, you can pay."

"You can even pick where we go."

He paints surprise across his face and follows me out the door.

3

May 1991
Cedar Falls, Iowa

Dr. Connor is a sport psychologist and UNI professor who's had the same office for the last 10 years. The office is a renovated dorm room reflective of recent remodeling. The small size of the room cannot be disguised, but the yellow walls are updated with wallpaper. The furniture, consisting of a round coffee table, a bookshelf, a standing lamp, and two plants, provides coziness in what might otherwise be a sterile environment.

The interoffice door opens at precisely 3:30 p.m. In the entrance stands Dr. Connor, tall as the doorway itself, and mostly legs.

"Brown hair, blue eyes; using the description you gave me on the phone, I'm guessing you're Lisa," she announces.

"And you must be Dr. Connor," I rise to shake her hand. "Thanks for making time to see me. I know you have another appointment to get to soon."

"Not until 4:00, so we can at least get started today," she says, as she leads me into her private office where an empty chair awaits. It faces her desk, the top of which is organized into piles of paper several inches high. The piles are flanked by jars of highlighters, red pens, and paper clips.

"Excuse the mess," she says, and clears some space. "I have final drafts of research articles due to the publisher in a few weeks and this is the result of many long evenings."

"What is your research about?" I ask, glancing at the piles.

"I have a couple projects going on, actually." She lays both hands on her desk. "The one that's due soon is called Home Court and Hoops. It's the study of home field advantage on female basketball players' performance," she says and flips

11

through some of the papers.

"Were you a basketball player?" I imagine her height to be advantageous.

"I quit playing a long time ago." She leans back in her chair. "A lot has changed since I played the game."

"Like what?"

"Scholarships, opportunity, pressure—or perceived pressure. So much more is on the line now than in those days. We're seeing more female athletes struggling with issues like that than we used to. My research uses female basketball players as subjects, but it could be any female athlete, really. Or male, for that matter."

"Sounds complicated," I say.

"Human behavior usually is," she agrees. We sit in silence for a moment. "So," she begins, and emits a deep sigh. "You know something about me. How about you?"

I consider the question carefully. "I'm not sure where to start. I guess I should tell you that I'm a wrestler. I train with my former high school team—Cedar Falls High—and sometimes with the UNI's team."

She nods her head but her expression does not change.

"My Dad is the psychologist for the UNI wrestling team— I guess you knew that."

Dr. Connor folds her hands. "Yes, I know. He's very well respected in the department. He also teaches the marathon class, right? The one featured in *Runner's World* last month? Fantastic stuff."

I smile. "I'm real proud of him."

"And he sure is proud of you. He talks about you and your twin a lot."

"I know it. Every time I meet up with his students on campus, they ask me what it was like to be a human guinea pig. All harmless experiments, of course."

She chuckles. "How does your mom feel about the experimentation?"

"They're divorced."

Dr. Connor shifts in her chair. "I guess that answers that question."

"Oh, don't worry about it. That happened a long time ago; they've been friends since then." I glance around the room for a moment. The geometrically patterned wallpaper distracts me.

"Rorschach tests?" I joke, gesturing to the wall.

She glances at the wallpaper and then at me. "Triangles."

I nod uncomfortably and the smile fades from my lips

"You were saying?" She gets me back on track.

"Anyway, that's how I knew about you; my dad mentions people in the department sometimes."

Dr. Connor repositions her legs but does not speak. She seems to sense my stalling tactics.

"The reason I'm here is that I'm having some trouble at the tournaments I've been wrestling in so far."

She nods again. "What kind of trouble are you having?"

I sigh, embarrassed to tell her how bad it really is. "I get nervous." I chew on the inside of my lip. "Really nervous."

"You mean like butterflies in your stomach? Or trouble concentrating? Or fatigue?"

"Yes," I agree.

"Yes to which?"

"All of them."

"I see," she says and nods again. "Is there ever a time when you don't get nervous?"

I think about it for a moment. "Not really. When I first started wrestling, it was just a twinge of agitation before a match or two. Now, for some reason, it is almost all the time."

"How severely do you experience these symptoms?"

"It ranges a lot. At tournaments, it's pretty bad right before a match."

"How about before practice?" she asks.

"Not nearly as bad. I just feel kind of edgy. Especially if there are boys at practice who haven't seen me before or if we scrimmage with a new team or something."

"What do you mean, 'boys at practice'?"

"Well, I train with boys."

She raises her eyebrows. "Do you ever wrestle girls?"

"Only a couple times a year. Most of the time, I train and compete against boys."

"Interesting," she says and sits quietly for a moment. "How long have you been wrestling?"

"A couple years."

"Did you play other sports before you took up wrestling?"

"Gymnastics, soccer, lacrosse, karate, rowing, track. I was a competitive bodybuilder for several years."

"Did you experience the same kind of anxiety with the other sports?"

I pause, considering the question. "Not really. I mean, I would get a little nervous," I shift in my chair, "but I had always been a pretty confident, calm athlete. Until now."

"What's different now?"

I shake my head. "I don't know. It just seems…" Again, I trail off, thinking about the importance of wrestling to me. "I just want to do well. I have to do well."

She nods, obviously considering her next move. Finally, she wheels her chair to a metal filing cabinet and pulls out one of the drawers. She fiddles through the folders, settling on one and retrieving a single sheet of printed paper. She slides it in front of me.

"First of all, I want you to know that you're not the first athlete with competition anxiety—that's what it's called, by the way. If you were the first, I wouldn't be conducting the research I just discussed with you and I wouldn't have this preprinted sheet." She smiles. "What I'd like you to do is read over the sheet and answer the questions honestly. The more honestly you answer, the more I can help you. Does that make sense?"

I nod in agreement.

"The questions are designed to profile the way nervousness physically manifests itself within you. You've told me a little bit about that, but I'd like to get a broader picture. Do you have any questions so far?"

"No, I understand."

"When we're done talking for today, fill that out and leave it with me. Give me a chance to look it over, and then at our next session, we can discuss the results." She leans back in her chair again. "Let's shift gears for a minute. Tell me a little bit

14

about how you got started wrestling."

I set the paper aside. "That seems like so long ago. My interest in wrestling really started because of my dad," I smile, thinking about him, and look out the window. "About twelve years ago, I guess I was ten, he took me to my first wrestling meet. UNI was wrestling Iowa."

"Did you enjoy the meet?"

"I hated it," I say, and we both smile at that. "That was surprising, because I love almost all sports. I guessed I wanted to be with my dad, though, and I'm sure that's why I continued to go." I take a deep breath. "Anyway, I started going to more and more UNI meets and pretty soon I fell in love with wrestling. USA Wrestling, the governing body for amateur wrestling in this country, began hosting the boys' Junior National tournament in Cedar Falls. Me, a couple of my friends, and my sister worked at it every year, keeping score for the Iowa team and stuff like that. Really, I volunteered to do anything just to be at the tournament. I used to sit up in the stands and watch all the athletes, wishing so much I could wrestle." I trail off, caught for a moment in that familiar feeling of longing. "Anyway, at that time, there were no female wrestlers— none that I knew of anyway. Finally, when I was in college, I just decided I had to try it for myself, regardless of what people thought."

"And now you don't care what people think about females wrestling?" she asks.

I deliberate for a moment. "I care more about wrestling."

She nods again and glances at the clock. "This might be a good place to stop for today. I do have to get to my other appointment across campus."

"I understand, " I say.

"Oh, and I almost forgot," she wheels back over to the filing cabinet and retrieves another piece of paper. "I need you to sign this confidentiality agreement. It means that our conversations are confidential, unless I believe that you would cause yourself or another physical harm, or that a minor has been harmed in some way."

I smile. "I'm not that nervous."

"I know," she chuckles. "Sign at the bottom."

I provide a careful signature.

"Don't forget to slip the other one through my mail slot in the door before you go today. She opens her calendar. "How does the same day and time next week sound?"

I shake my head. "Next week I'm at wrestling camp. How about the following week?"

She checks her calendar again. "I can do that," she says, and pencils me in. She gathers her briefcase and keys and rises to walk me back to the outer office.

"Just to clarify," I say, pointing to the confidentiality sheet. "That means you don't talk about our conversations with anyone, right?"

She studies my face. "It's between you and me, Lisa."

"Good," I say, and release a breath. "It would be pretty embarrassing for me if anyone found out that the daughter of the wrestling team's shrink can't keep it together."

She puts a comforting hand on my shoulder and strolls away.

I drop onto a couch cushion to complete the form. I read it to myself carefully as Dr. Connor suggests. *Review the symptoms below and place an X next to those you have ever experienced prior to or during competition.* I begin with the first item on the alphabetized list and read quietly to myself. *Abdominal discomfort.* I recall the trips to the bathroom just before matches, cramps, and constipation. Check. *Appetite loss.* I remember the times my nervous stomach keeps me from eating. I make a check mark next to the symptom. *Cold feet.* The extra pair of socks beneath my wrestling shoes. Check. *Cold hands.* My frigid fingers. Check. *Difficulty concentrating.* The inability to focus on the match and inability to ignore the self-doubt. My breathing accelerates as I read more quickly through the list. *Edginess... fatigue... heart palpitations... inability to focus... irritability.* Check, check, check, check, check. I read down the list faster and faster. *Muscle tenseness... racing heartbeat... racing thoughts... sleeplessness... slow reaction time... tense abdomen...* Check, check, check, check, check, check. My heart pounds as I mark the page, my pencil a sword, slashing Xs, revealing my weaknesses. *Teeth chattering; uncontrollable shivering; yawning excessively.* I throw the pencil across the room and it hits the wall. The paper remains on the table, taunting me, but displaying the inevitable. I have marked all the symptoms.

Hopelessness swells in my chest and through my limbs. *I can't give this to Dr. Connor. She'll think I'm crazy.* I exhale loudly and stare out the window at the UNIdome. The giant UNIdome, a massive covered structure built for athletic and scholastic events, was the site of the Junior Nationals wrestling tournament each summer. When the tournament week arrived, I would run for the stadium entrance and push on the revolving door. The vacuum it created sucked all the sound from the air and my gut ignited with the familiar twinge of anticipation. When the door completed its revolution, it thrust me into the vastness of the wrestling tournament already underway, roaring like a steam engine down a track at a hundred miles an hour. Scorekeepers and statisticians hurried about the 16 multicolored wrestling mats covering the football-sized floor. Whistles chirped and timing buzzers erupted. Referees dressed in white scampered to catch every wrestling move on their mats. The announcer's voice thundered through the arena, calling wrestlers to report for their matches. "Knight, Iowa; Jackson, California; report to mat three. Knight and Jackson, mat three." Volunteer workers scurried across the floor to the head table with match results. This head table, located on the east side of the dome, housed reporters and announcers. A room hidden mysteriously away from this main area harbored the statisticians who posted the coveted results along the dome walls for eager fans to view.

The acoustics of the temperature-controlled dome muted the enthusiastic voices and blowing whistles, but it could not conceal the energy. Wrestling coaches lined the mats like military officers, some of them yelling hysterically at athletes about to lose their matches. Other coaches sat quietly in their chairs and celebrated the success of their stars. I sat in the highest row of the dome, the metal of the hard bleacher seat cold against my back. Wrestlers' screams and referees' whistles echoed in the emptiness of my heart. The longing to wrestle ached deep in my gut, stretching far beyond the sprawling mats.

I recall the longing now, clear as Iowa sky. I approach Dr. Connor's closed office door and grip the form, covered in Xs, now a reflection of me. I close my eyes and slip the sheet through the slot. Through the glass, I watch it float quietly to the floor.

4

June 1991
Colorado

One week later, I descend the jet bridge in Denver to attend my first wrestling camp. I drag my oversized duffel bag down the ramp that opens to the main terminal and to an anticipating crowd awaiting loved ones and visitors. At the end of the ramp, a man dressed in wrestling regalia peers at me. It is Coach Tom Wagner, the head wrestling coach at the high school where the camp will be conducted. He is a man of shorter than average height and has the rounded shoulders of a former wrestler. I suspect he is prematurely gray and what remains of his hair barely covers the sides of his head. His face is spherical with a button nose and his eyes are medallions of blue ice. The two of us are a billboard with our sweatshirts, caps and printed T-shirts. On the pocket of his shirt, blue embroidered letters spell out Greenwood High School—Head Wrestling Coach.

Our conversation is plagued by only a few awkward silences during the drive from the Denver airport to Greenwood, a small community securely tucked away at the top of a mountain road where the camp will be held. We engage in benign conversation as we arrive at the home of Mark Hernandez, another local high school coach, and his wife Maria. Coach Wagner had arranged for me to stay with this couple during camp week. This is common practice in the sport; local families and coaches frequently offer housing to the athletes attending training camps or tournaments in their area. This practice was due in part to lack of funding for the sport; wrestlers are well known for getting by on shoestring budgets and relying on the kindness of fans and coaches. My father had housed wrestlers every summer when Laurel and I were growing up and now I humbly accepted the generosity of this family.

Coach Wagner honks the horn announcing our arrival as we approach a massive house built in brown, grainy wood, with immaculate doublewide picture windows, and a loose pebble circular driveway. The honking horn summons Coach Hernandez and Maria to the outside landing. Coach Hernandez is a bulky, square-framed man with waves of black hair painted on a boxy head. His mate is the female version but with a lighter complexion and copper hair.

Coach Wagner hops out of the driver's side to be greeted. I stand removed from the three of them as they smile and laugh. When the initial greeting is complete, Coach Wagner presents me as Lisa, the girl wrestler. I make sure to use a firm handshake.

Dinner is already on the table when Maria invites us inside. The four of us gather around a rustic, square wooden table. I smell spices and peppers, powerful enough to melt cold steel. As we stand around the table commenting on the smells, the screen door opens and reveals Charlie Henry. My admiration for accomplished wrestlers borders on extremism to be sure, and this case is not different. Charlie was training for the Goodwill Games that year, and he moved from his native Oklahoma to the Olympic Training Center in Colorado Springs to train almost year round. He is no taller than I am but his energetic presence and his accomplishment in the sport makes him impossible for me to ignore.

"Where have you been?" Coach Hernandez asks Charlie.

"Yeah, we're starving," Coach Wagner adds with a smile.

"Sorry to make y'all wait." Charlie wipes sweat from his forehead. "Getting in a quick run before dinner." He approaches Coach Wagner. "Hey, buddy." He pats him on the back. "Great to see you again."

Coach Wagner returns the embrace. "You too."

"Another run?" Maria asks and shakes her head. "That's the second one today."

"Just a few miles," Charlie responds as he rounds the table to me. "We have a visitor I see," he says, "Sorry about the sweat." He wipes a palm on his shorts and then presents an open hand. "You must be Lisa," he says with confidence. "Charlie Henry." He extends his hand and looks at me through serious eyes. Despite my history with wrestlers at multiple levels of celebrity, I struggle to keep my hand from quivering.

"Pleasure to meet you." It is all I can get out of my mouth at the moment. I didn't realize that Charlie would be staying at the house, too.

Charlie pulls out a chair at the dinner table and the rest of us follow. We pass heavy wooden bowls and glass plates around the table as Coach Hernandez spurs most of the conversation about work, the neighbors, the weather. Charlie and Coach Wagner chime in with talk of wrestling camp. Camp begins tomorrow, Monday, and lasts through Saturday with a half session on the final day. Sessions will be twice daily, one in the morning and again in the early afternoon. I get lost in thoughts of camp when Charlie interrupts my daydreaming.

"This is your first camp, right?" Everyone at the table looks at me. My mouth is full of food and I reach for my water glass to speed the swallowing process.

"First one. I was actually planning to attend a different camp originally, but yours came highly recommended." I consider that the diplomatic answer.

"I'm glad to hear that," Charlie says with genuine humility.

"Have you conducted many of these camps before?" I take another sip of water.

Charlie nods. "I've done a camp in Greenwood every summer for the last five years."

"We've got a lot of good wrestlers coming from around the state this time, Charlie," Coach Wagner adds. "It's gonna be a good one." He switches gears. "Lisa, are you training for something in particular?"

"Working for a spot on the National team," I say.

"Really," he says as a statement. "That's quite a goal." Coach Wagner smiles.

"How many other girls do you train with?" Maria asks.

I chew some more food. "Actually, none. I train with guys."

She raises her eyebrows. "You train with boys? Why is that?"

21

The others stir in their seats.

"Unfortunately, there just aren't any females wrestling where I live to do it any other way. If I want to wrestle, I wrestle the boys."

An awkward silence looms.

Finally Charlie speaks. "Do you beat them?"

"I've never beaten a boy at a tournament. I have in the practice room, though."

Charlie picks up a forkful of Spanish rice and tilts his head. "Camp should be interesting," he says, placing the rice in his mouth.

I am alone, lying on the firm mattress over the metal frame of my guest bed and I stare out the window at a dark, star-decorated sky. Coach Wagner left hours ago and the others are surely sleeping soundly. Tomorrow morning's session is only eight hours away and I feel a familiar stir in my gut. I try to sleep but visions of wrestling moves roll around in my head like a rat on a wheel. It reminds me that by this time, Dr. Connor has seen my questionnaire with all my symptoms marked. I wonder what she thinks of it.

The alarm startles me at 7:30 the next morning and I am momentarily disoriented. When my brain catches up, the significance of the day sends the butterflies swirling in my stomach. I dress quickly in workout shorts and a sweatshirt and wander out to the kitchen to find Maria cooking again.

"Scrambled eggs are almost done here. Any interest, honey?"

I welcome her gentleness in this unknown place and have an appetite for that much more than the food. "That's very generous of you," I say, buying time to formulate a kind rejection. "I find it a little hard to eat before wrestling, though; I hope you understand."

"Of course, sweetie. How about some juice?"

I picture the acidic juice rolling around in my empty stomach, but accept it anyway.

"Sounds great," I say and her face becomes a giant grin as she pours fresh squeezed orange juice into a plastic cup.

"You guys better go," she says, glancing at the clock. Coach Hernandez appears from the hallway and Charlie flanks him.

"You're right, honey," he agrees and kisses her cheek. With my juice in hand, I grab my gym bag and step into the brisk mountain air. The sun shines across the tops of the mountains and reflects shades of blue and brown. They are capped at the top with glaring snow. The majesty of the huge ridges strikes me. It has been a while since I focused on anything else but wrestling.

Coach Hernandez drops us at the driveway of Greenwood High School. I stare up at the brick structure outside the gym door. Faintly, I hear playful screams and yells of adolescent boys inside and wonder if any of them have wrestled a girl before.

"In here," Charlie says, his hand on a set of double doors. I take a deep breath and Charlie pulls on one of the metal handles. "Consider it your home for the next week."

I nod and shift my gym bag to relieve the tension on my shoulders and step inside. The rest happens in slow motion. The door swings wide and hits the wall behind it. Unfamiliar faces turn toward the commotion. The door shuts behind us like a drawbridge and echoes throughout the cavernous gymnasium. I stare into the open space.

The room is a converted cafeteria with three mats covering a linoleum floor. On the back wall, windows overlook the schoolyard and the school bus driveway. Vending machines with juices and soda are pushed against the walls and share the space with rolling cafeteria tables.

Several wrestlers are already in the room and rush to greet Charlie. Their ages appear to vary from about 11 to 19. I am not much older, but the only one wearing a sports bra. Some of the fathers in the room smile at me curiously; others avert their glances when I meet their eyes.

In a matter of minutes, my abdomen muscles tighten like a rubber band. The cold air strangles me. I feel the pressure mounting; more campers file through the gym door, more stares and whispers, more commotion. The pang of self-doubt creeps in. It feeds on itself. The more I try to ignore it, the more powerful it becomes.

I retreat in search of a place to regain focus. Through the cafeteria exit I find a carpeted hallway and a restroom off to one corner. I take refuge in it, lean my back against the far wall and breath fresh air through my nose, hoping to wash the toxic feelings away. When the acute anxiety seems under control, I douse my face with water in the cracked white sink and look into the vanity mirror. How many times I have been here or someplace like it, hiding away in solitude, trying to relax tense muscles, and talking to myself, all the while knowing I must wrestle in spite of it.

I wander back to the wrestling room to find the group assembling in the center of the room. They sit cross-legged or kneel in front of Charlie, eagerly awaiting his first words. I take a place in the back row and watch as Charlie silences the whispers.

"I'd like to welcome all of you to Greenwood wrestling camp. My name is Charlie Henry, a graduate of Oklahoma State University—"

"Go Cowboys," Coach Wagner yells from the back of the room.

Charlie agrees and gestures in some kind of traditional hand signal. He continues by reciting some of his accomplishments, including an all-American at OSU, a member of the Sunkist Kids wrestling club, and the 1988 Goodwill Games champion at 105 pounds. The group claps spontaneously after this humble but confident introduction.

Charlie politely silences us by getting right to work. "The first thing we'll do this morning is run the lake. It's only three miles, so no jogging. I want every one of you running as fast as you can." All the younger wrestlers rush to the door, fearing they will be last to finish the run, but Charlie is a roadblock. "Wait a minute, wait a minute." He places playful hands atop the heads of the eager young campers to hold them back. "When we return, we'll start wrestling, so make sure you're warmed up." Charlie releases the stampede and the crowd charges the door.

The challenge unleashes the competitiveness in me. I spot a lanky wrestler whose legs are almost twice the lengths of mine. Keeping up with him is a sure bet to keep me in front.

We burst through the doorway into the June air. I trample the ground beneath me, forcing the adrenaline through my veins. I stay in close proximity of the long-legged wrestler who is setting our pace. We round the first corner and cross a narrow wooden planked bridge. The steep uphill pumps blood through my legs. I panic momentarily, knowing I have set out too fast. A sudden change swells through the wave of runners: wrestlers begin to drop back and soon I am part of the leading mob. Mountain air rushes through me, stealing some of my breath and restricting my lungs. Still I target the wrestler slightly ahead of me who is relaxed, leaping with the stride of a buck, and hardly straining. I lengthen my gait to keep up with him, though I am clearly beyond my limits. The wood bridge rumbles like thunder as we roar over it.

The beginning of the second mile is marked by a low-grade incline on a paved road but my pacer gains traction and speed. The incline feels like a ninety degree hill as every step rips away at my legs and the altitude constricts tighter on my throat. I accelerate to keep from losing sight of the pack as we round a tight corner. Sweat droplets mature into steady streams of perspiration but I have no energy to wipe them away. I have lost the feeling in my legs as numbness and lactic acid replace fresh blood.

"Don't let her beat you," I hear one wrestler gasp out to another as my legs churn, one over the other. The pacer is at full speed now, pounding through the miles. My skin shivers in shock. I am nauseous, and the numbness resonates through me like the last ring of a church bell.

My first road race seems ages ago now. When my father was just beginning his running career, he had invited Laurel and I to run a race to see if we liked it. It had seemed so important to him that I try. Throughout the race I had hung back with the slower runners; I was just 12 years old and not expected to perform any miracles. At mile six, I emerged over a hill to see my father at the bottom, long since finished, but waving my sister and me toward the finish line. A burst of adrenaline rushed through me as I ran toward him, faster and faster. I never looked back.

Miles of road running and years of training separate me from that moment now. The long-legged wrestler pumps his arms and lurches forward in preparation for the finish. Charlie is atop the final hill, which marks the finish line, coaching us on. Galloping wrestlers nip at my heels and I hear the rhythm of their breath matching my own. I gasp and fight through the pain. The altitude squeezes the air from my lungs like a python. I am tripping over myself, falling forward more than running, as the pacer's last steps blast past Charlie with mine following shortly after.

I adjust my gait to slow down and my legs quiver as a final reminder of the torment. Panting in spite of what feels like collapsed lungs in the Colorado mountain air, I clasp my hands above my head and circle back around to see Charlie cheering on the rest of the wrestlers, whom I have beaten to the finish line.

I walk in purposeful wide circles to cool down and debate about what feels better, being in front or being finished. A thought creeps in and for a moment, it seems absurd. But it is persistent. *Why do I care so much about winning?* More circles, more cooling down. Eventually, the question, and perhaps its answer, spiral away.

I return to the gym with the small group of wrestlers who have finished first. I feel my muscles cooling down and the tenseness setting in again. I stay in motion, keeping the blood flowing through my body. I adopt my wrestling stance and, with my hands bent loosely at my sides, squat up and down slowly to keep my muscles loose. My breath begins to return to a normal pace. I am almost cooled down, and distracted by momentary comfort.

Lisa Whitsett

"Where did you learn that?" Troy Sway, a star wrestler of Greenwood's team, is glaring at me. Hostility seeps through his tone of voice.

"Learn what?" I continue squatting in my corner.

"That motion." He imitates the level change but modifies it by thrusting his hips outward with emphasis.

I continue the squatting, determined to ignore him, while the other wrestlers who flank him laugh at his sexual reference. Peripherally, I see the group hustle away to another corner. I shake my head, slapped by his immaturity.

Coach Wagner enters through the far doorway and passes Troy on the way in. "Making some new friends?"

"Not exactly," I say, reaching into my duffel bag for a dry T-shirt.

"Forget about it. They'll get used to your being here."

"It's okay if they don't," I shrug, and surprise myself by meaning it.

My mouth is dry from the run. I join a line of wrestlers marching down a hall to a set of water fountains. I overhear some of the parents talking to Charlie as they huddle nearby.

"Troy Sway looks tough again this year," one of the fathers mentions to Charlie.

"Yeah, he does look good." Charlie bends down to get a drink of water. "Doesn't he have an older brother who wrestles, too?" He wipes dripping water from his lips.

"Yeah. Nick," the father continues. "But I'll be surprised if he does well this year. He lost districts two years ago and he never fully recovered. I don't know what happened to him. He just kind of fell apart after that."

"His dad's pretty upset about it," another father adds. "He had big plans for his sons. Scholarships, sponsorship—the whole thing. It isn't quite working out the way he had hoped with Nick. But Troy's still on the right track."

I drink slowly from the water fountain and listen to the story of this family. Scholarships, sponsorship; it sounds so appealing. The boys don't have too much to worry about, it seems.

27

"How did you like the run?" Charlie asks the group as we huddle back together.

"Too hard!" Some of the younger campers yell out to Charlie.

He laughs. "Too hard?" He grabs the instigator and turns him playfully upside down. The boy giggles while the blood rushes to his head. His friends laugh with good nature.

"Anyone else think the run was too hard?" Charlie asks.

No one admits to it and Charlie sets the boy back down on the mat.

"Who's ready to wrestle?" Charlie asks.

The crowd of wrestlers burst into a roar, and I feel like if I don't start moving I'm going to explode out of my skin.

"All right, let's start wrestling then," Charlie announces and demonstrates the first series of moves. He introduces several takedowns and soon dismisses us to practice on our own. Most of the campers have come with teammates or friends and have been paired up long before camp. Those who did not have a pre-selected partner quickly find one. I am the only wrestler in the room without a partner.

Without drawing attention to myself, I approach Charlie. He is reaching over two wrestlers, contorting their bodies into correct position.

"Would you mind partnering with me to drill this?" I ask.

Charlie gives a final word of instruction to the pair and then rises, looking around the room. He places his hands on his hips and wrinkles his brow.

"I thought I counted an even number of wrestlers," he says, confused at how I am left standing by myself.

"You did," I offer, gesturing to a threesome in the corner. "Look, if they're uncomfortable, that's okay." I shrug. "I just want to wrestle. "

He weighs the options. "Hold on a minute," he offers, and trots to his bag to pull a ring off his finger. He returns quickly and we drop into our wrestling stances. We drill for several minutes before Charlie stops me.

"You need to relax," he says with a serious look on his face. "Your whole body is way too tense." He grabs my arm and pulls on it. "Look at that. You're like a piece of wood."

I defend myself. "I'm concentrating."

"On what? He challenges me. "You should be at about twenty percent of your maximum power. We're just drilling. The point is to teach your muscles the moves through repetition. You have to let them do the moves, and do them correctly. If you're tense, they're busy doing something else." He drops back into his stance. "Try again."

I breathe out resolutely and drop into my stance again. We dance around each other, dropping and turning, back and forth on the mat. He stops me again.

"All right look," he starts. "You're like a mannequin."

I put my hands on my hips.

"Let's try this," he says and looks up at the clock. "You have three minutes to hit as many moves as you can. I'll defend you at about twenty percent of my maximum—remember, we're only drilling, so concentrate on your form. Don't stop moving. If you stop moving, you start over again, and we add one minute for every time you stop. Ready?"

"Ready," I say and drop into my stance.

I shoot, throw, and turn him. Before one minute is up, sweat beads on my forehead. My muscles begin to fatigue slightly. I shoot again and take Charlie to his back. We jump back to our feet and I throw him again.

"Two minutes to go," he says, hardly out of breath. "Don't stop." This play continues until Charlie calls time. I drop back and sit on my heels, my legs burning and my chest heaving.

"How do you feel?" he asks.

I nod. "Relaxed."

Charlie offers a hand and pulls me back to my feet.

When the afternoon session begins, I notice a stout man, perhaps forty years of age draped in photographic gear in the corner of the room. He has a receding hairline and thin reddish mustache that matches the red in his T-shirt. The top is paired with khaki pants and no belt. Rugged boots complete the ensemble. Throughout the afternoon, his camera clicks and the flash flickers in my eyes. Eventually the reporter pulls Charlie away for an interview and my partner disappears.

I scan the room for someone to continue working out with. Hoping that the novelty of my being here has worn off, I settle on two boys. As I approach, I hear them discussing the intricacies of a move we had learned earlier in the day.

"I thought we were supposed to step with the inside leg first," one of them asserts.

"I thought it was the other way around." The other demonstrates.

"No way. That doesn't work. You end up backwards if you do it like that."

They stand with their hands on their hips.

"It's the inside leg first," I offer, after watching for several minutes. The boys look at me.

"What?" one of them asks.

"It's the inside leg," I say and face one of the boys. "Like this," and I demonstrate.

"See, I knew it," one boy agrees, giving his partner a friendly shove.

I take a risk in the wake of this connection. "Can I drill a little with you guys?"

I recognize one of them as the lanky boy I followed in the front of the running pack. Until now, I had only seen him from the back, but the lengths of his legs were unmistakable.

"You almost killed me in the run this morning. I could hardly keep up with you."

"You should have tried a little easier. We were running to stay ahead of you," he says, and circles to face me in his wrestling stance.

Soon the reporter returns Charlie to the group.

"Found someone to drill with?" Charlie asks me, patting the lanky wrestler on the shoulder.

"Yes, sir," I answer.

"Can I borrow you for a minute?" Charlie continues. He introduces me to the newspaper reporter, still loaded down with his camera.

"I'd like to find out a little more about women's wrestling," he begins.

"Happy to help. As long as I can drill with these guys when

I come back," I say, and Charlie makes sure of it.

With that assurance, the reporter and I descend a short stairway to a lobby, engaging in small talk as the commotion in the wrestling room fades behind us.

"Have you done many interviews?" he asks, arranging his papers.

"Not really."

"I appreciate your willingness to talk to me." He pulls out his spiral pad and a pen. He begins with some basic questions about my getting started in wrestling.

"Most people think I mean the World Wrestling Federation or the Gorgeous Ladies of Wrestling," I explain. "Or they ask me if I mud wrestle."

He shakes his head while he scribbles on a note pad. "What do you say to them?"

"I tell them they should know better; I wrestle in Jell-O." We both laugh and he scribbles some more. This seems to be the kind of information he is looking for: some kind of juiciness that wraps neatly around the gender issue. "Some people are supportive of women's wrestling, and other people are threatened by it."

The reporter makes a face. "Why do you think that is?"

I shrug. "Maybe people who don't see their own potential are threatened by others' potential. Or maybe they just need some time to get used to seeing females on a wrestling mat."

He is furiously scratching notes on his legal pad. "Is that the hardest part about wrestling for you? Others' disapproval?"

He leaves me an easy way out. I know the hardest part of wrestling for me: keeping my head together. But I dare not say it.

"It's a challenge," I say instead.

I reappear a half hour later to find that Charlie has divided the wrestlers into three lines to run sprinting drills.

"What are we doing?" I ask, joining the end of the line where my partners are.

"Relay," the long-legged wrestler says. "The last line to finish has fifty push-ups. The second line has twenty-five."

"What did the reporter ask you?" His friend says.

"How boys react to wrestling me," I say, purely for shock value.

"What did you say?" they ask, almost simultaneously.

"What should I have said?"

"Probably that it's weird wrestling a girl at first," one says.

"But then after a while it's not a big deal," the other adds.

I nod in agreement. "That's about what I said." I take off, sprinting down the length of the room.

The afternoon session is nearly over and I revel in the satisfaction that my first day of wrestling camp has gone well. Only a few campers remain and I overhear Nick Sway and his father playfully arguing about him being scared to wrestle me. Eventually, Nick wanders over, dragging his feet.

"My dad wants to know if you'll wrestle me."

"Your dad wants to know or you want to know?" I smile to take the sting out of the question. I find it such an odd challenge and I feel sorry for him. He really has no choice; it is his father's wish, not his.

"Do you want to wrestle or not?" His tone is biting and his pitiful reality strikes me. Nick must be hoping that I will decline his request, since he cannot decline his father's. His only option is to abide by his father's wishes. On another day, I might have declined, but I am not willing to risk being called timid or scared. That is *my* pitiful reality.

I agree to wrestle him in folkstyle, the primary style practiced in high school and college and therefore, by most boys, though I wrestle freestyle. Folkstyle differs in some ways from freestyle; specifically, folkstyle uses a different kind of mat wrestling and the scoring system is different.

Knowing this, I still approach the mat with Nick, his father still smirking and heckling his son. Butterflies swirl in my stomach as Nick's father sounds the whistle. We explode at each other, circling and bounding, evading each other's moves. We lock up with each other but I am unable to gain any leverage.

Nick's forearms are twice my size and the rest of his body is the same.

I know I am not as strong as he is so I attempt a throw to get the match over with. I hit the move quickly. It surprises Nick who curses as he begins to lose the upper hand. We are sweating though, and his arm slips out from under me. I choose not to attempt the throw, fearful of ending up in worse position.

Nick's father yells to him. "You better watch it, son. She almost launched you," he taunts. Nick does not answer and returns to the center of the circle.

Right off the whistle, Nick drops his level and shoots in on me but I sprawl back. He fights and pushes for the points, and he is barely able to score as we go out of bounds.

"Come on, Nick," his father yells. "You should have finished that off with a pin and had this match wrapped up."

Nick waves him off.

We start back in the center of the mat. Because Nick had the upper hand on our way out of bounds, I am required to start in a position in which I am already down on the mat. Nick's father sounds the whistle to begin wrestling again and I explode out from under him. I have almost escaped his grip when he lifts my body and tosses me to the ground. My elbow breaks a violent fall and pain rings through me. I scramble to get back to my feet but for a moment I am off balance. Nick exposes my back to the mat and holds me there, which wins him two points and the match when his father calls time.

We are sweating and panting when we rise from the mat to shake hands. Relief blankets his face as Nick extends his hand to shake mine. I reciprocate and pain shoots from my elbow to my shoulder. I look down to find my elbow three times its normal size from the impact of the fall. Nick points to this grotesque extremity, growing by the second. I hobble to the side of the mat to shake hands with Nick's father, who proclaims our match exciting. I hear him providing post-match coaching tips to his son as I proceed to the training kit.

Coach Wagner sees my bulbous elbow and trots over.

"What happened?" He kneels down next to me and touches

my arm. I pull it away instinctively and fiddle through the training kit for an ice pack and a bandage.

"Landed on it wrestling Nick." I smile through the pain. "That's what I get, I guess." I continue rummaging through the kit, unhappy with the only wrapping tape I find.

"We should get you to a doctor to take a look at that," Coach Wagner offers. "I can run you up to the emergency clinic right now if you want. It's not far."

"My insurance won't cover it. Besides, there's not a whole lot they can do unless it's broken, and I don't think it is. Don't worry about it. I'll be fine."

"It looks pretty bad." Coach Wagner examines my elbow more closely. "You sure you don't want to go to the doctor?"

"I'm sure," I insist, and begin wrapping with the tape.

"What were you doing wrestling Nick anyway?" Coach Wagner asks. "He's at least thirty-five pounds heavier than you are."

"I got caught up in the moment, I guess. Couldn't resist the challenge," I say. I see Nick from across the room, shining in his father's approval.

"Can you still wrestle this week?"

"If you don't mind me being wrapped up while I do it," I say, raising the elbow.

"Makes you look tougher anyway," he says and smiles.

I nod knowingly and continue wrapping.

Five days later I return home, my first wrestling camp successfully under my belt. Coach Wagner had sent me home with the newspaper article written by the reporter I spoke to. I read each word carefully and find no misquotes. Charlie calls me a quick learner, very mature, and says I have all the aspects of a top competitor.

I toy with the article and sit back on the couch. I recall the inability to relax during practice, the trips to the restroom to regain focus. He sees aspects in me of which I am not completely convinced. Unmistakable waves of uncertainty wash over me as the discrepancy between Charlie's view of me and my view of myself collide.

5

June 1991
Cedar Falls, Iowa

"Pretty scary, isn't it?" I ask, as I sit before Dr. Connor again, two weeks to the day after our first meeting. She has my completed questionnaire in front of her. "Have you ever seen a more anxious athlete?"

"Yes, I have," she says. She sets the paper down. "Let's forget about the actual check marks for a moment. We'll go back to them in a minute."

I straighten up, grateful for the temporary pardon.

"Tell me what it was like to fill this out," she continues.

It's as clear right now as it was then: the hopelessness at checking all the symptoms, the frustration, the embarrassment. I drop my head and shift in my chair, but I am unwilling to say anything. She leans back and clasps her hands in her lap, waiting for me to speak. Several moments tick by before she finally breaks the silence.

"Let me show you something." She visits her filing cabinet and pulls out a sheet of paper. It is the same form I had filled out, but someone else has completed this one. She slides it in front of me. "What do you think?"

"It's covered in check marks. It looks almost exactly like mine."

"Yes, it does," she agrees.

"This was one anxious athlete."

"Yes, she was."

"Did she get better?"

"No, she didn't," she says and emits a deep sigh. "Partly because she would never talk about it. She stopped playing her sport after a while."

I chew on the inside of my lip. "I don't want that to happen to me."

"I don't either."

I push the paper back to her. "I didn't like how I felt when I filled it out."

"Tell me more."

"I didn't like the reflection of me." I offer a weak smile to replace the displeasure of admitting that. But the discomfort still unnerves me and I rationalize in order to keep a safe distance from it. "Wrestling is an environment where being in control is really important. Being strong and tough, mentally and physically, is part of what will make me successful. This paper makes me look exactly the opposite. It makes me look weak."

"So these are signs of weakness to you," she clarifies.

I concede with a nod. "I spent a lot of energy at camp trying to cover them."

"How did you do that?"

"By wrestling people a lot stronger and heavier than me."

"And? How did it go?" She asks.

I hold up the taped arm. "Not bad until I twisted my elbow off."

"Ouch. Anything serious?"

"I don't think so; it's fluid or something. The bump's going down already."

"How did it go besides the elbow? The nerves?"

"Not so great." I think back to the first night. "I couldn't sleep at night at all. All I could do was watch wrestling tapes in my head—wrestling moves over and over again—until I was too tired to keep my eyes open."

"For some athletes, visualization helps calm them down and feel more in control."

I shrug. "Sometimes it does works that way for me, too. But more often, the visualization makes me more nervous. When I close my eyes, the images just appear, even when I'm trying not to think about wrestling."

"Why do you think that happens?"

I shake my head. "I don't know."

Dr. Connor seems to look right through me. "I'd like you to rehearse something that might help you stay a little more focused. What I suggest is called progressive relaxation. It's a method used to create awareness of tension in your body by contracting and relaxing your muscles. Most people start with the smaller muscles in the body first and move to the larger ones, but there are many ways to do it. The method helps you learn to control both."

"I didn't know that's what it was called. I do that already; I borrowed an audio tape from my dad."

"How many times a week do you listen to it?"

"It depends. At the least once, at the most three times a week."

"Let's build on what you're already doing, then. Practice at least once a day, and let's add two things to it: a word and an action. First, pick a word that you can associate with getting focused and relaxing. What would you like it to be?"

I chew on my lip.

"I find myself repeating the word 'focus' a lot. That might work."

"Good. One more thing: we need an action to pair with the word that'll help trigger the relaxation. Pick an action that gets your attention."

I shrug. "Could I clap my hands together?"

"Sure, that's good. When you're practicing your relaxation, say your cue word to yourself when you exhale. At the same time, clap your hands together. She demonstrates. "Say the word in your head and clap, every time you practice."

"How long will it take before I notice a difference?"

"I'd like to see you again two weeks from today and we'll see how it's going."

"I can't. I'll be in Washington at wrestling camp."

"Another one?"

"Nationals are coming up soon. I have to be ready this time."

She pulls out her calendar again. "We're getting into July already. Three weeks from today?"

"See ya then, Doc," I say, and disappear through the doorway.

6

July 1991
Cheney, Washington

Through the mist of a humid afternoon, my taxi driver roars into the dormitory parking lot of Cheney University in Washington. I grab my bag from the back seat and step out onto the paved road as the driver pulls away. The driveway leads to a set of concrete steps and then to a set of double doors, which open to another stairway. A cafeteria table displays various flyers and posters advertising university student activities and scholarship information. Another set of double doors is propped open on the left side of the room exposing a lounge with faded blue wallpaper. Inside it, cozy couches and a reclining chair invite the tired and weary.

I take a few steps into the room when I hear a husky, rumbling voice in the corridor. I have never seen Myron Roderick before today, but I knew he would be at this camp, and I am sure this is he. Myron Roderick had been a three-time NCAA champion in college. He was only twenty-three years old when he accepted the head coaching position for Oklahoma State University and was the youngest wrestling coach ever to win the NCAA wrestling championships. I watch Coach Roderick saunter through the hallway, hunched over slightly at the waist indicating not his age but his athletic history. Five young men in their late teens follow him, carrying on and shouting about nothing in particular.

"Coach Roderick?" I ask.

"I didn't do it," he jokes, as wrestlers hang on him, wrapping playful arms around his neck.

I hold out an open hand and introduce myself. The boys scatter like cockroaches. "I guess I need to check in?"

"Ah, Lisa. Our girl wrestler." He peers over glasses, inspecting me. "How do you do, young lady?" His accent is thicker than Midwest beef and I imagine rows of cowboy boots lining his closet. He shakes my hand and asks me to follow him to a nearby table on which lie several pieces of paper, some pencils, and several keys.

"Here's your meal pass and your room key," he says, handing me a laminated card and a door key on a string. "Keep it around your neck unless you're wrestling. That's how the campus folks know you're allowed to be here. Breakfast, lunch, and dinner are in the cafeteria down the hall. The first session starts tomorrow morning at 9:00 in the wrestling room, and we go again at 3:00 p.m. and then at 7:00 p.m. every day for the next week."

"Thank you, sir."

He hands me a liability waiver. "Can ya sign this for me?"

I take a moment to read the form.

"You been trainin'?" He asks as I digest the legal terms of my not suing anyone if I break my neck.

"Yes, sir." I sign the form and hand it back to him. "Every day."

"Better be tellin' the truth," he says with a smile. "Cause we'll know the first day if you're not." He winks at me and ambles away.

Three other wrestlers and I wait in the lobby for the elevator going up. We step in and soon after, they engage in that familiar banter that emerges with adolescence. It is an awkward stage, somewhere between demanding attention and wanting to appear disinterested.

The boys exit on the fourth floor and I ride alone to the seventh where I find my room. I drag my suitcase down a hall of painted off-white walls and greenish carpet. I hear no voices and no sounds except the elevator doors closing behind me. My extra large gym bag bounces against my leg as I arrive at my room and unlock the door.

The institutional metal door swings wide and creaks open to reveal a small but adequate dorm room. Two single beds line either side of the room and built-in drawers make up the far wall. I drop my bag on one of the beds, a temporary storage spot, and lock the door behind me.

I open the curtains to reveal a window peering over the dormitory courtyard and a field of grass. The sun descends behind a hill and leaves an orange wake. Coach Roderick's words ring through my head and the pressure to prove what I can do weighs heavily on me.

I wash my face and hands, and replace my key and meal pass around my neck. I return to my bag to change into work-out clothes in preparation for an evening run, and find my relaxation tape. Promising myself I'd run immediately after, I arrange the pillows and sheets comfortably and lay down on the bed. I insert the tape into my Walkman and when it starts, I hear the familiar sound of a female voice suggesting I concentrate on my breathing. It's the last thing I hear before falling into a deep sleep.

I awake at 3:00 a.m. and dash to the bathroom. My Walkman, still attached to me by earphones, drops to the ground. The tape, the batteries, and the cassette player scatter about the floor. I barely make it into the stall when I vomit violently. My heart races; sweat beads on my forehead. I clutch the sides of the toilet bowl for another round and my stomach wraps in knots. I drop to the floor next to the bowl and lay my head against the cool wall until the knots subside. I sit dazed, stomach cramping, and try to figure how I would have contracted the flu in such a short amount of time. I drag myself back to my room, fearful of vomiting again but too tired to keep my head up.

Morning comes and nausea awakens me, but it is too late. I have already missed the start of the first session by several minutes. I pull myself to the edge of the bed, bracing myself in case I have to dash to the bathroom again. I am frantic as I grab my wrestling shoes and run down the hall and seven flights of stairs.

I am panting when I get to the bottom. I do not know where to run next. I remember the student information table in the front lobby. I run to it and find a giant map illustrating the campus. Clearly marked on the left side of the map are two gymnasiums, one with a large indoor track facility and the other with a large swimming pool. I choose the gym with the track hoping a wrestling room is nearby.

Nausea nags at me when I finally reach the training room. I saunter through the double doors trying to compose myself, hoping the beads of sweat on my forehead do not give me away. The first glimpse of hundreds of other wrestlers slaps me with adrenaline. A crowd of young males, ranging in age from about fifteen to eighteen, bands around Coach John Smith.

I had first met John Smith when we were both in high school. He and another young wrestler had come to stay with us for the week prior to competing in their national tournament. As UNI's team psychologist, my father had often offered to lodge some of the wrestlers at our house for the week in order to help keep them more focused than they might be if they had to stay in the dormitory.

A couple nights before the tournament started, my father had asked each of them about their wrestling goals.

The first answered. "I'd like to win this tournament and then go to a good wrestling school." My dad offered some encouraging words and then turned to John.

"How about you?"

John was polite and soft spoken. He looked out from under long eyelashes as his feet dangled off the end of the couch. "I'm going to be a world champion, sir."

There wasn't much to say after that.

John Smith emerged as one of the most successful American wrestlers in history. He won the 1988 and 1992 Olympic freestyle gold medals in his weight and was a four-time world freestyle champion.

Now at camp he stands in a circle of wrestlers. I clench my jaw to tame the nerves but self-consciousness pierces me. Every set of eyes weighs heavy as I draw closer. I can hear that they have begun introductions of the coaching staff already, and I breathe sporadically as I approach the group wishing I had a less conspicuous entrance. My stomach swirls with nausea again and I beg not to throw up just yet.

When I am close enough, I kneel in the circle like the others. In the purest tradition of wrestling, no one in the group sits or lies down lest they be scolded for being lazy. Instead, all wrestlers are stooped on one knee; taller wrestlers are in the back of the circle standing.

Coach Smith describes an intense camp agenda as Coach Roderick paces around the perimeter of the mat, keeping an attentive eye on the wrestlers and his staff. Compared to Greenwood, this camp has a more intense, focused undertone and it resonates through the serious, focused expressions of the coaches, the staff, and the participants. I like the change, but I get the feeling that if someone steps too far out of line, we will all pay the price.

We waste no time following Coach Smith's first round of technique and we pair up to drill the moves he has demonstrated. When the crowd breaks to find partners, I wade through the inevitable sea of the boys' fears.

"Don't let the girl kick your butt," I overhear.

I laugh to myself knowing how inexperienced I am, but my insides twist up and I hope to find a partner before Coach Roderick has to assign me one. I spy a wrestler who looks to be my weight, standing alone. He sees me coming but does not move.

"Need a partner?" I ask as I approach.

"I promised that guy over there I'd be his partner," he says, pointing to no one in particular.

I glance in that direction. "Which one?" I press him to be specific.

"I don't know where he went," he clarifies. "He was going to get his head gear." Coach Smith appears just in time to neutralize the infuriation.

"Good to see you again, Lisa." His presence is commanding and I am embarrassed by my admiration.

"You, too," I answer quickly and we shake hands.

Coach Smith turns to the boy. "What are we waiting for over here?"

I stare at the wrestler, wondering what his excuse will be.

"I'm waiting for my partner," he suggests.

"You have a partner right in front of you," Coach Smith answers, and gestures to me. "Problem with that?"

The wrestler shakes his head. "No, sir."

"Didn't think so." John walks away and leaves us in the corner. I smile to myself, grateful for his support.

In my periphery I see others staring. Beyond them I feel the massiveness of the gymnasium, sprawling and expansive, and I am a tiny speck of dust in its imposing space. My head spins, blurred and unfocused in the giant chasm between the wrestler in front of me—ready to rip my head off—and the rafters of the enormous arena.

"Wait a minute," I back off and my partner sneers at me. I turn away and stare off into nothingness, remembering what Dr. Connor had prescribed. I take a deep breath, then another. *Focus. Focus. Focus.* I repeat it to myself, but the words bounce against a wall of self-consciousness over and over again. *Focus. Focus. Focus.* I try again, this time with my eyes closed. I feel too silly to pair the clap with it, knowing this will call attention to me.

"Do you want to drill or not?" my partner shouts at me. I ignore him and repeat. *Focus. Focus. Focus.* I feel the fog lift just a little, and my lungs breath air with more ease. I turn back to my partner without answering. Instead, I drop into my stance and pummel against his bodyweight. Well-earned sweat steadily drips from my body as the morning becomes afternoon.

I drag myself back to my room at the completion of the first session, grateful for not vomiting during practice. I shower and fall asleep in a towel but wake around 1:30 p.m. to throw up again. Between dry heaves (I have been unable to eat from nerves), I think about the consequences if I do not show up at the next session. All the doubters who say I can't take it and I am not tough enough to handle it would appear to have won. Coach Roderick will think I had lied to him about training. No one would care whether I was puking or not. All they would see was that I wasn't there and my worst fears would come true. I simply could not let it happen.

I dig through the dorm drawer and find the local Yellow Pages. I call the number of a walk-in clinic a couple of miles away from campus. I figure if I run the two miles, I might be able to see the doctor and still make it back for the afternoon session at 3:00. I waste no time dressing and am running down the road before anyone sees me sneak off campus.

Outside the clinic doors, a bulletin board posts the hours of the clinic and the doctors who practice in the building. Inside, a waiting room hosts fabric-covered chairs. Magazines ranging from *Sports Illustrated* to *Parenting* lay in disarray on a square coffee table. On one side of the room a receptionist sits behind a glass divider. I approach her and she hands me some paperwork, which I complete with a shaky hand. The nurse calls my name shortly after.

The nurse says nothing as she shows me into a room to take my blood pressure. I explain my symptoms to her, which she notes on a chart. She announces that the doctor will be in momentarily and I wait again. I lie down on the paper-covered patient bed and stare at a sterile ceiling. This is not how I had planned to spend wrestling camp.

The clock ticks closer and closer to 3:00. Just then, the doctor knocks on the door and enters. He is a middle-aged man with a stocky build and a serious expression. A cotton button-down shirt and khaki pants peek out beneath his white coat. He holds my chart in one hand and a pen in the other, asks questions, and jots down notes. After I finish reciting my symptoms, the doctor announces that I probably have a stomach virus of some kind. I leave the clinic with a brown bottle of giant pills and 20 minutes to get back to camp.

The exertion of my running back to campus feeds whatever is making me ill, and I vomit again when I get back to the room. Disgusted with the way camp has gone thus far, I ignore the cramps in my stomach, gargle some mouthwash, and force one of the pills down my throat.

I vaguely remember the doctor mentioning something about drowsiness from the medicine, but I had been preoccupied at the time and did not listen closely. This negligence turns out to be unfortunate, as I struggle to keep my eyes open during the 3:00 session. I am crammed into a weight room with the other wrestlers as we curl barbells and squat weighted bars for an hour. The temperature in the room has escalated from the body heat, and I feel like I am in an incubator. Drowsiness weighs on me.

"Circle up!" Coach Smith blows a whistle and we abandon our weightlifting posts. Coach Tim Jackson, his protégé, flanks him. "You've got one half hour of conditioning. Treat this like the last minute of a wrestling match when you're tired, you're fatigued, and you want to quit. Push through it; this is where champions gut it out." He hands his whistle to his second in command. "This is Coach Jackson; I expect you to treat him with the same respect you give me. Let's get to work." Coach Smith leaves, shutting the door behind him.

Coach Jackson's white blond hair and newborn baby face are deceiving. He blows his newly acquired whistle and commands us to drop to the floor. "100 pushups. When I blow the whistle, drop halfway down but stay in pushup position," he commands. "When I blow the whistle again, drop down to starting position, but do not—I repeat—do not, let your body hit the ground. You will start when I tell you and you will go on my count. Do not go faster than my count. Understand that if anyone drops to the ground, we all get to start over."

Wrestlers groan under their breath.

"Any questions?" This is a rhetorical question of course. He blows the whistle and barks out the order. "One!"

The torture is well underway and by the fiftieth pushup, my arms and chest quiver. Whimpers and winces sound from all parts of the room, but I remain focused on the goal, the only way I know to get through it.

"Ninety-nine!" Coach Jackson blows his whistle. "Half way down. Get your butts down!" Several wrestlers sound as if they are nearly crying, trying to keep their bodies from touching the ground. Ruthlessness invades the room. Sweat drips off my nose and pools in a small puddle below me.

"One hundred," he yells finally, and I recruit the last muscle fiber I have to push to the position. I sit back on my heels, my chest muscles pumped full of blood. The blood in my body helps a little with the fatigue, but I still struggle. The room is filled with groans, overshadowed only by Coach Jackson's whistle sounding again. He herds us into the hallway for more work. Even I can't help cursing under my breath.

We conclude the evening with the notorious wall-sit: squatting in a ninety-degree angle against the wall and holding the position until we are told to release it.

"We'll do this for five minutes. Don't let me see any of you giving up before that time." The whistle blows again to begin our time.

I observe several wrestlers groaning and shifting their weight, cheating themselves out of a full effort. Some of them collapse after only two minutes, which is met with scorn from Coach Jackson. Blood burns in my quadriceps, hot and fiery. Coach Jackson paces up and down the line of wrestlers, barking out the command to sit lower to some of those who are struggling to keep their positions. He finally blows the whistle at the end of the five minutes.

He dismisses us with a final word of advice. "Sleep it off; tomorrow's gonna be a long day." I disband with the others, dropping to my duffel bag for my medicine. Coach Jackson sneaks up behind me. "We've got a little stud right there," he whispers to me in a lowered voice on his way by. I stare at him as he saunters away, twirling his whistle around his finger. He glances back at me but I am too fatigued to decode his tone.

I dig through my bag for the bottle of medicine and scan the label, which reminds me that severe drowsiness may occur. That is an understatement. I consider my options, and choose nausea over the fatigue. I dump the medicine into a nearby trashcan, tossing the bottle back into my bag in case I need to fill it when camp is over. I heave my bag over my shoulder and drift back to my room. Uncertainty circles overhead; the challenge of a full week of camp threatens to take a bite out of me.

7

July 1991
Cedar Falls, Iowa

I return from the Washington airport to my shrilling phone. I drop my duffel bag and run for it, feeling the leg bruises I earned at camp.

"It's Tom Wagner with Greenwood High School. I know we haven't talked a whole lot since you were here at camp, but I have a proposition for you." I listen as he explains the circumstances surrounding an open coaching position at Greenwood. "Do you have any interest in coming out here to coach our team?"

"I don't know what to say." I pace around the living room.

"If you decide to come, you'd get some really good experience here."

"Coach, it's very flattering. Really. But I wrestle Freestyle; Folkstyle isn't even my specialty. In fact, I don't have a specialty; I haven't been wrestling that long."

"I know, I know—" he starts.

I interrupt him. "I'm almost the same age as they are, too; getting their attention as a coach might be a little challenging. Even if I do, they already know a whole lot more than I do."

"Not all of them." He breathes a deep sigh. "Look, I've been coaching for a long, long time. Every year I say it's going to be the last, and every year after that, I sign up again. I figured as long as I'm going to go another round, I might as well make it interesting."

"I guess that's one way to look at it."

"Besides that, you have a chance to make history. As far as I know, you would be the first paid female high school wrestling coach."

I smile. "I have to think about it."

47

"Don't think too hard before you say yes," he jokes.

I hang up, my heart leaping in my chest.

I help Dad clear the table from dinner he made for us while he washes the dishes. He pushes remnants of meatloaf with a ketchup glaze and baby green peas into the garbage disposal.

"And you think this is something you want to do?" he asks, continuing the conversation I started with him about coaching at Greenwood.

"Yeah, I do." I tidy up the dining room table. "Everyone I've ever talked to says coaching is a good way to improve your own technique."

"Well, you'd be a good coach, I'm sure of that. This is a pretty big change, though, too. It means moving there for the season, postponing school—"

"Just for six months," I remind him.

"Oh, I know you'd go back. I'm not saying that." He changes his tone. "You might be able to save a little for your student loans anyway. Do you get paid by the month?"

I hadn't bothered to ask. "I don't know when I get paid."

"Where will you be living?"

I hadn't asked that either. "Don't know."

"How will you get around?"

I shrug. "Not sure yet."

He turns off the faucet and rubs his hands on a dishtowel. "Any of these details seem important to you?"

"Not compared to the opportunity. I can figure it all out when I get there."

He sets down the dishtowel and shakes his head. "How can a father who plans everything down to his breakfast every morning have an offspring as spontaneous as you?"

"Mom says I'm being impulsive."

"That's another word for it."

We talk for another thirty minutes about my decision, which I had actually made before I got to his house, until we've exhausted the subject.

"So how are practices going?" He asks, setting a cup of

decaffeinated coffee in front of me.

I sip from the mug. "Really good. I worked out with Coach Briggs yesterday in the UNI room. He spent almost the whole practice with me."

"He told me that, actually. Says you're really strong."

I smile. "At least the weights are paying off."

"What do you mean 'at least the weights'? Is something wrong?"

I wish I hadn't let it slip out. "No, not really. I just...I expect a lot of myself, I guess."

"Wonder where you got that," he says with sarcasm, knowing he passed his tendencies directly on to me. But it is more than high expectation and discipline that I inherited, and he knows it. A marathon runner for years, he is the picture of mental toughness: invulnerable, strong, and controlled. He preaches it and he lives it. And so do I. Anything less is simply not an option—the stakes too high, the alternative too unimaginable. That fact alone makes the anxiety so much more shameful and embarrassing to me.

"How was camp?" Dr. Connor asks, when I see her at our scheduled appointment.

"The technique instruction was amazing. My head is packed with new stuff."

"How about the nerves?"

"Not so good."

"Did you have a chance to listen to the tape and practice your cues?"

"More times than I care to count." My head is still lowered. "I think I'm getting worse."

"What makes you say that?"

I shake my head. "This is so embarrassing." I laugh out of awkwardness. "I can't believe I'm telling you this."

Dr. Connor says nothing; she sits in silence and waits. I chew on the inside of my lip. I tell her about flu symptoms and visiting the doctor, about the medicine he gave me, how it made me so drowsy, and how I chose not to take it.

"When I was packing up Saturday to leave camp, I found the bottle from the medicine. I start thinking back to the first day of camp, and it occurred to me that my nausea was completely gone, despite not taking the medicine, and had been for several days."

Dr. Connor nods.

"Then I thought back through the entire week. The second day was about the same as the first—I was still throwing up—but it wasn't quite as bad. The third day I didn't feel quite as sick. The fourth day I felt much better and by the fifth and sixth days, I felt back to normal."

"But you hadn't taken the medicine?"

"Right. At the same time I was thinking about the flu symptoms, I noticed something odd."

"What did you notice?"

"I noticed that the first day I was really, really nervous that I wouldn't wrestle well."

"Go on."

"The second day, I was actually wrestling really well. I was still nervous, but I was doing okay."

"What about the third day?"

"We had kind of a mock dual meet where we had to pick teams and stuff. I was chosen second out of 200 boys that were still left."

"I think I see where this is going," Dr. Connor says. "Your symptoms weren't the flu?"

"I don't think so."

"Anxiety?"

"The worst it's been so far," I confirm.

Dr. Connor takes a deep breath but does not seem shaken. "I guess we have some more work to do then, don't we?"

"We better do it fast," I say.

"Why the hurry?"

"I won't be living in Cedar Falls too much longer. I've accepted an offer to coach Greenwood, Colorado's high school wrestling team. I leave in two months."

8

July 1991
Cedar Falls, Iowa

"When will you be back?" Steve asks me, as he sits down on his couch.

"I'll be back in February, when wrestling season ends." I join him on the couch. "Don't worry, the time is going to fly by. I hope you understand. I really have to do this. Besides, you'll be too busy with your own season to even think about it."

He grabs my hand and kisses it. "I can't believe I only met you two months ago and now you're moving away."

"It's just temporary, I promise. I really don't think I can pass this up. It could be really good for me."

"I know, I know," he says. "I just...I don't want you to forget me."

My heart melts at his soft brown eyes, his warm hands. "I won't forget you, I promise."

He smiles. "You better not."

Steve and I met at a hole-in-the-wall college bar on The Hill one Saturday night after a wrestling meet. I watched as he twirled a pool cue in his hand and juggled a drink in the other as he playfully engaged with his friends, also UNI wrestlers. He was unusually shy and more introverted than most of the wrestlers I knew. I learned later that was also an excellent pool player, enhanced by his knowledge of physics, his college major. It goes without saying that I lost all my quarters on the pool table the night we met, and I don't regret it.

That was a few months ago and since then, we have spent the majority of our time together. I find him easy to care about. I fear sharing that with him, though, figuring that once I do, I'm vulnerable to being hurt. So I'm hiding for now. His gentleness seeps into me, creating a longing to be near him but simultaneously telling me to run away. I don't understand any of it.

"The longer I stay here, the worse this will be. I better just get it over with and go. My dad's expecting me for dinner in an hour or so anyway." We rise from the couch together and he hugs me.

"Don't let them push you around out there, okay?"

"Do I seem like the kind of girl who would let that happen?" I say, and playfully wrestle with him.

He resists at first, but then drops into a wrestling stance. "Okay, tough girl, let's go," he says and begins to use some force.

Steve is 145 pounds and I am barely 105. More importantly, I have been wrestling for two years and he for more than fifteen. I am outmatched in more ways than I care to count, but I continue the challenge anyway. Soon I start to push and pull him as if we are in a real match. He laughs at me, spurring me on, until I am using all my power. He is still laughing playfully but begins to engage in the match.

"We're gonna need more room for this one," I say, and break free to run upstairs. Steve chases me. We are pummeling each other in the center of a room, which is under construction, filled with power tools, hammers, and ladders. Despite Steve being in complete control, I am trying my hardest to take him down.

"Had enough?" Steve laughs as I am rolled in a ball.

"No way. Not until I win this," I say, determined to get out from under him.

"Come on, Lisa. I'm killing you."

"I don't care. I still have something left."

Steve has complete arm and most leg control but I spy a metal ladder folded against the wall. I kick at it and try to grab onto it for leverage. Steve is behind me, still laughing, and does not see the ladder collapsing under the pressure. The ladder hits me square in the face and then crashes to the floor sending tools, plywood, and sawdust into the air.

Steve immediately kneels beside me. "Oh my God." His face is pallid and his breathing irregular. I keep my face covered.

"Just let me just see it!" He cries, gently prying my hands from my face.

I blink my eyes several times trying to clear my head; the events leading up to that moment become blurry. "What does it look like?" I demand.

Steve doesn't answer directly. "Oh, honey." He touches the top of my nose lightly, examining it closely. "You better take a look," he suggests.

I stand up to go to the bathroom mirror and the room spins wildly.

"Do you want me to come with you?" He says, the shakiness in his voice undisguised.

"No, just give me a second," I demand. I shake off the dizziness and finally make my way to the bathroom. Firmly supporting myself on the sink, I peer closely into the oval mirror.

"Don't get scared when you see yourself," he shouts from the other room.

A yellowish green tint blankets the bridge of my nose and a definitive break in the skin indicates that my nose is probably broken. Dark circles are forming under my eyes and I consider the impact this could have on my training. I feel the crushing blow of disappointment and the wave of dread not far behind it.

When I am able, I drive to my father's house, periodically checking the rearview mirror to see the various stages of my nose injury. It looks worse; a bump the size of a walnut emerges from a collage of black and blue.

I rap on my Dad's screen door.

"Come on in, honey." He shouts from the inside. "The door's open. I'll be there in a second." I slip through the unlocked door and rush straight for the hallway mirror. Not pretty. When I hear my father's bedroom door open, I turn my face away. I head for the refrigerator and grab the water pitcher, momentarily covering my face.

"Hi, Dad," I say, with my face turned away from him.

"Hi, Honey." He kisses my cheek. "Ready for dinner? I'm buying."

I realize I cannot hide this from him forever, but the consequences scare me. Finally, I set the pitcher down and my father immediately scrunches his face. He places a gentle hand on either side of my face and examines my nose.

"How did you do this?" He asks, turning my head from side to side to get a closer look.

"At wrestling practice today. I got kneed in the face when I took a shot," I lie, hoping the logic makes sense. I cannot tell the truth about the injury, embarrassed at taking the match with Steve so seriously. Instead, I start building up the tough athlete story, one that my father knows well and that we both buy into, heart and soul.

"Must have been a hard shot," he says. He looks more closely. "I think your nose is broken. You got it pretty good there, Honey," he points to the bump on the top. "Feel like a trip to the hospital before dinner?"

We sit in the doctor's office for several minutes before he finally comes in with the x-rays. He wears a traditional lab coat and a stethoscope around his neck. He introduces himself to us and with one practiced motion, he slips the x-rays onto a lighted clipboard mounted on the wall.

"Let's see what we've got here," the doctor says, examining the pictures closely. "There it is," he announces. "Broken in two places. Here and here." He points to two small hairline fractures in the x-ray of my nose.

"That's what we thought, didn't we, Partner?" My father confirms. I slide off my stool to see the fractures, curiously interested in the injury.

"Yeah, we did," I say, running my hand over the x-rays.

"Can you tell me how this happened?" The doctor asks.

"During wrestling practice." I stammer a little, wondering if the doctor will find the lack of logic in the story. "I took a shot on my opponent and he brought his knee up at the same time. We collided."

The doctor is unsatisfied. "Did it knock you out?" He asks, scribbling on a chart.

"No," I say, shaking my head.

"But you must have hit pretty hard," he concludes.

54

My father pipes in. "She's very strong. And tough. Wouldn't surprise me at all actually if she hardly felt it," he says. Guilt sets in immediately as my father defends me.

"Did you stop practicing after that?" the doctor presses.

I waver for a moment. If I say yes, I risk my father thinking I wasn't tough enough to keep going. If I say no, the doctor might suspect something. "No, I didn't stop. It didn't really seem that bad." I shift in my chair as the doctor approaches me with a lighted device.

"A collision like that would have stopped a lot of people cold," the doctor says as he peers into my eyes with the bright light.

"It just didn't really hurt that bad at the time," I pull away from the light. "It hurts now, though, that's for sure."

"Headache?" the doctor suggests.

"A big one."

"Are you feeling sleepy at all?"

"Very," I answer.

The doctor scribbles some more notes on my chart.

"Well, Lisa, you have definitely broken your nose," he pulls the x-rays from the wall. "You also have a concussion. You're going to need to stay off the mat for a couple weeks to let the nose heal and to give your head a rest."

Panic rises in my chest. I wriggle in my chair. "I really can't take a couple weeks off. I have a big tournament coming up and then Nationals soon after. I've been training all year."

The doctor glances at my father. "I can't make you take the time off, but I can tell you that in order for the injury to heal, it needs time."

I shake my head and my father puts his arm around me. "It's okay, Partner. We'll get you to the tournament. A few weeks won't kill you."

A tear wells in my eye and I sniffle it away. Even the guilt I feel from lying is eclipsed by the disappointment about time off the mat.

At the doctor's suggestion, I sleep at my father's house that night as a precaution. I awake in the dark several hours later, groggy and disoriented. I push myself up and feel dampness on my pillow. I switch on the nightstand lamp to find some kind of clear fluid covering the pillowcase.

I consult the materials the nurse gave us during our visit. *If the patient finds fluid of any kind leaking from the nose or ears, call the hospital immediately.* Feeling light-headed and dizzy, I stumble out to the kitchen and dial the telephone. As I am explaining my symptoms to the nurse, my father emerges from his bedroom. I had been trying to hide this from him, thinking I might be making a big deal out of nothing. In the middle of the phone call with the nurse, I faint, sliding down the wall in a heap. My father rushes me back to the hospital; this time, we go to Emergency.

A doctor enters the office and introduces himself to Dad and me. He has a graceful manner and appears to be of East Indian decent. He pulls a pen from the pocket of his blue scrubs, opens my chart, and emits a lengthy sigh.

"Lisa," he begins, "the discharge you found on your pillow is cerebrospinal fluid – brain fluid." My breathing turns shallow. My father's eyes widen. "The fact that it is leaking from your nose and ears indicates that you have cracked your Cribiform Plate. The Cribiform Plate is a bony structure that separates the brain from the sinus area. The impact of collision was simply too much for the plate to absorb, and it fractured."

He waits for a reaction from us, but both Dad and me say nothing.

"The doctor who originally treated you may not have seen it in your x-rays because it was hidden by the breaks in the nose," he says. "It is a relatively small fracture in the plate, but it is a very serious injury."

Silence floods the room. The overhead lights buzz.

"Will I have to stop wrestling?" The words barely trickle from my mouth.

The doctor takes a deep sigh. "For a while, yes."

"How long?" I squeak it out.

"About ten weeks."

"You have got to kidding."

"It is quite serious, Lisa. There are potential threats to you with an injury like this." He stands up and crosses his arms. "And, though cases are rare, one of them is meningitis."

My father lurches forward in his chair. "Meningitis? Christ, that could kill her."

"What is it?" I shout. Dad rarely sounds alarmed or startled. Hearing his reaction sends my blood racing.

The doctor speaks calmly, trying to diffuse us. "Meningitis is an inflammation of the brain and spinal cord tissues. Bacteria or a virus of some type causes most cases. And yes, some types can be fatal if the symptoms are not treated quickly."

My heart pounds through my chest.

The doctor wheels a chair over and sits directly in front of me, his knees wide and his hands clasped. "The bacteria that tends to cause meningitis exist in one of every ten people at any given time. People carry the bacteria in the back of their noses and throats without ever realizing they are there. However, in a few cases, the bacteria overcome the body's immune defenses and pass through the lining of the nose and throat into the blood stream. Once in the blood, they can infect the brain tissue and spinal column. You are at risk for this because of your injury." He studies me. "You need to let the injury heal. That means no wrestling, no workouts, for ten weeks. At the end of that time, if it is healed, you can slowly resume your workouts again."

"And what if the plate doesn't heal on its own?"

The doctor elevates his head and gives me a serious stare. "It means we would have to surgically repair it."

A lump rises in my throat and tears form. The thought of having my head shaved and my skull repaired did not appeal to me. But the alternative seemed even worse at the moment. The year's training for the tournament is for nothing.

An hour later, my father walks me out to the parking lot, holding my hand. Before I go to the passenger side of the car, he stops me.

"Come here," he says, and I see fear in his eyes. He wipes

away a tear from my face. "It's okay to cry. This is scary." I turn into him and absorb a hug, reveling in his comfort. I wonder if he would be as compassionate if he knew the truth about how the injury really happened. I fear he will not be. I keep the fear and the truth to myself.

When we arrive home, I phone Steve.

"What happened?" he asks when he answers the phone. "I was worried when I didn't hear from you right away. Are you okay?"

"Sort of. The injury is pretty bad." I lay my head on a pillow and explain the situation. "I told the doctor it happened during practice. Please promise me you won't tell anyone how it really happened. I'm too embarrassed to tell anyone."

"I won't say anything," he assures me. "Does this mean you don't go to Colorado?"

I turn over onto my side. "No, I'm still going, but I'm probably not going until October. It does mean I miss the tournament. That's the part I can't seem to let go of."

Steve scoffs. "Your brain is leaking through your nose, and you're worried about wrestling?"

Rage pumps through me. The least he can do is try to understand. "First of all, brain fluid, not my brain, is not leaking through my nose." I rise resolutely from the bed in one action and scoop up the materials the doctor sent me home with. "And secondly, it does not surprise me that a wrestler like you—on a university wrestling team with dedicated coaches, brand new warm-ups, and all your tournaments paid for—is shocked that I'm concerned about missing one of two women's tournaments a year." I crumple up the hospital brochures, throw them in the waste can, and whirl into the kitchen, pacing like a caged tiger. "I've trained all year for this tournament. I've sweated through camps and three-a-day practices for it, so yeah, I'm a little upset that the doctor has ordered me to miss the tournament and has laid me off the mat for the next two months." I throw gestures as if he is standing before me, not noticing the clear fluid that has dripped onto my lip. "While your season continues along as normal, you can think of me sitting on my ass doing nothing except getting fat and out of shape. And then, when I am able to wrestle, you can think of me again, when I hope and pray that the money that USA Wrestling has allotted to the women's program—which, by the way, is half of what they allot to the men's program—is still available." My gait is faster now and my breathing has turned shallow. "Yes, I am a little concerned about wrestling, Steve, and I am sorry you can't understand why."

My head throbs. Fluid drains from my nose and I wipe it with a tissue while silence looms on the other end of the line. I realize what I've done a moment too late; the damage is already done.

"Steve?" I drop into a chair. "Are you still there?"

"Done yelling now?" he asks.

I sigh. "I'm sorry. Really, I'm sorry. I just—"

"You don't have to explain," he says. "I got enough of that."

"I'm sorry."

"I just called to see if you were okay."

My heart melts. "Thanks."

"Give me a call sometime," he says. Finality looms in his tone.

"Please don't be mad at me. I didn't mean to yell at you," I say, wishing I could take it back.

"I'll talk to you later," he says, and hangs up.

I wander back into the bedroom and drop noisily into the bed. I shake my head at my outburst, put my hand over my face, and lay my head against the pillow. When the world seems to have disappeared, I turn the fluid-soaked pillow to the other side, and fall asleep.

Several days later, I stand outside Dr. Connor's door, pondering exactly what to say to her about all of this. I do not want to reveal the truth about how the injury happened, but I feel guilty for lying. She is trying to help me, after all. Finally, I rap on the wooden door.

"What the hell happened to you?" She stares at my nose, fading from black and blue and turning more yellow.

"Wrestling." It's a half-truth. I drop into my usual chair.

"Is it broken?" She says and leans over the desk.

"In two places. Plus I cracked my skull."

She puts her hand over her mouth.

"I'm leaking brain fluid through my nose and ears."

"Oh my God," she cries. "Are you going to be okay?"

"It looks like it. But the doctor says no wrestling for more than two months."

"The tournament?"

I shake my head and then stare out the window.

"You must be very disappointed."

"That doesn't cover it." I sit for a moment as discomfort gnaws at me. "I guess we can look at it this way. I have plenty of time to practice not getting nervous."

"Are you still going to Colorado?"

"Yeah, I'm still going."

"How are you feeling about it?"

I shrug. "Inadequate."

"Why is that?"

"Most of them are better wrestlers than I am, but they don't know it. I'd prefer they didn't find out."

"You need to be better than they are to be a good coach?"

"No. I need to be better than they are to be a good wrestler."

Dr. Connor says nothing.

"Can I come back to see you after the season ends in February?"

"I'd be happy to see you. What will you be doing with your-self between now and when you leave for Colorado?"

"Not much, actually, and it's going to kill me. I can't wrestle, of course, but beyond that, I can't even work out. No biking, running, no lifting weights. It'll be the longest I've ever gone without working out."

"You sound a little panicked."

"Wouldn't you be?"

"Not considering the alternative."

"Which is?"

"Well, I'm not a medical doctor, but I believe there are several. Meningitis is one of them, isn't it?"

"Yeah, that's what the doctor said."

"Pretty scary stuff."

I wave her off. "I just can't imagine what I'm going to do for the next ten weeks."

"You'll think of something." She rises to walk me to the door.

"See you in February?"

"I'll be here," she confirms.

9

October 1991
Colorado

Wrestling gear slides across the back seat as Coach Wagner takes a sharp turn into the driveway of Greenwood High School. The pavement is slippery with a covering of snow and frozen ice beneath it. I hop out of the front seat and follow my new boss through a side foyer to the main school hallway. It resonates with buzzing voices of high school kids rushing to class before the bell stops ringing.

I trail after Coach Wagner down a long, well-lit hallway to a row of offices. We round the corner to the largest office of all with a glass door boasting Principal John Hall's nameplate.

Coach Wagner pauses. "Don't let him intimidate you. He's a big guy, but he's got a soft heart."

I take a deep breath and he raps on the door.

Through the glass we see Mr. Hall hunched behind an oversized oak desk. His droopy jowls vibrate as he exhales; each breath seems more difficult than the one before. He clutches a pencil in a stubby, callused hand and peers over bifocal glasses pushed down to the end of his nose. We knock again and Mr. Hall jumps, his eyes nearly rolling back in his head. He signals us to come in.

"Hallo, Coach. What can I do for you today?" He references Coach Wagner but he looks at me.

"Just wanted to introduce someone to you, sir," he gestures to me. "This is Lisa Whitsett, our new wrestling assistant."

Mr. Hall pushes his chair back and stands to receive my handshake. "That's quite a grip you have there," he says, glancing out over his spectacles.

I suspect he is patronizing me and I struggle to contain

myself. "It's a pleasure, Mr. Hall," I say, still pumping his hand. "I've heard a lot about you." I say it even though it isn't true. I am trying to make Coach Wagner look good.

Mr. Hall's chest rumbles with a gruff chuckle as he pushes his glasses back up onto the bridge of his nose. "Oh, have you now," he says, raising an eyebrow at Coach Wagner. "And what exactly have you heard, young lady?"

"All good things, I promise."

"She's diplomatic, alright," he says, and lumbers back to his seat. "I like that. We could use a little more grace in our coaching staff."

"You think she's diplomatic now," Coach Wagner adds, "but you should see her on the mat." They talk about me like I'm not in the room, exchanging comments about my capabilities and my experience. I stand between the two of them, turning my head left to right throughout their banter.

When they are satisfied they have exhausted the subject of my being at Greenwood, Mr. Hall pulls out a file drawer, and retrieves several sheets of paper. "You'll need to sign those and return them to me by the close of the school day on Friday. We also need a copy of your driver's license and social security card."

"Yes, sir." I clutch the documents. "No problem."

He turns to Coach Wagner and speaks in a quasi-hushed tone. "Have the wrestlers seen her yet?"

"Some met her at wrestling camp, you know. But she hasn't been to practice yet. Today is the first day."

"I see," Mr. Hall grumbles. He rests his hands on his protruding belly and leans back in his chair. "Welcome aboard, Lisa. Good to have you." He turns to Coach Wagner. "This is going to be a very interesting wrestling season. Don't you think?"

"That's the plan, sir," Coach Wagner agrees and shuts the door behind us.

We march down the carpeted hallway, our strides matching. The drama surrounding my being at Greenwood annoys me. Mr. Hall calls it interesting, a curious euphemism. Irritation and self-doubt mix inside me, the latter most challenging to overcome. I internalize the feelings, wondering for a moment if there's something wrong with me for loving this sport so much. Reason comes to the rescue; I tell myself to simply let it go.

I spend the next few hours loitering in Coach Wagner's office reading over the materials that Mr. Hall has given me. I sign each of the documents and sniffle periodically through my nose; though the fluid no longer drips from it, the habit remains. I wipe my nose with a tissue to be sure. I wad it up and violently throw it in the wastebasket. I have been off the mat for almost ten weeks and the absence is killing me. I have done no physical activity during this time: no running, no biking, and certainly no wrestling. Dread is interrupted by Coach Wagner's gentle knocking at the door.

"Wake up, Lisa, " he says. "It's time to meet the boys."

I trail Coach Wagner into the blue matted wrestling room. White cement walls enclose the space. At the far end several wrestlers, already cutting weight for the season, ride stationary bikes. Girlfriends loiter by the wrestling room awaiting attention, which they never receive. Posters of famous wrestlers and clippings of wrestling news garnish the perimeter of the room. In my peripheral vision, I see two of the wrestlers whispering and glancing at me.

"It would seem I've been spotted." I say.

"They'll get used to it," Coach Wagner says. "I did."

"Yeah, but you wanted a female coach. Can I say the same for them?"

"Don't worry about it. Once they see what you can offer them, they'll want your help." He changes the subject. "How do you like the room?"

"I really wish I could wrestle today," I respond, knowing that will not be happening for another two weeks. I reach up and touch the bridge of my nose.

Coach Wagner blows his whistle announcing the beginning of practice. I try to pay attention but my legs quiver with anticipation. Several minutes pass before he mentions my presence, and I hope that the wrestlers have satisfied their curiosity before I step up to the plate.

"I'd like to introduce our new assistant coach for this year. Her name is Coach Whitsett and she's joining us from Iowa."

I see Nick and Troy Sway among the crowd and wonder what they must be thinking.

Coach Wagner continues his introduction. "She was the national runner-up last year in her weight class. Some of you know her from camp this summer; we're lucky that she's back with us for the season. Lisa, would you like to say a few words?"

I smile and address the group of young men. I provide a brief synopsis of my wrestling background and athletic history, hoping to win some approval by the end of my monologue. I want to conclude by announcing that this is a dream come true and if anyone spoils it for me I'll have him in a sling. Instead, I explain that for two weeks or so I am not able to wrestle due to a head injury. I conclude with the conventional glad-to-be-here.

For the remainder of the first day, Coach Wagner instructs while I assist the less experienced wrestlers. Momentary awkwardness plagues a few of them when I touch them to position their arms or legs properly, but my mind is preoccupied with cautiousness as flying feet and bodies come dangerously close to my face. In my periphery I see Troy making a mockery of most of his opponents; no one in the room matches his talent or experience. Nick looks on with less fire in his eyes and I wonder what thoughts hide behind them.

My sigh of relief trails the last wrestler out of the room and the door shuts. I lay down on the wrestling mat, warm now from body heat. Colorado's high altitude continues to cause my heart to race.

"We had a great practice today," Coach Wagner beams.

I cannot help but smile back. "Especially for the first day," I agree. "You have some great wrestlers."

"*We* have some great wrestlers," he emphasizes. "You're the coach, too, remember?"

I smile. "Right."

"The guys seemed to really take to you when you jumped

right in to help them. They need to see you on the mat as much as possible." He pauses, waiting for my reaction.

"I'll be out there rolling around as soon as I can, believe me. It's driving me crazy," I say, feeling pressure to heal faster.

"Oh, no, I know that. I just mean that the more interaction the guys have with you, the better. You have a lot to add to these practices, especially when we start showing takedowns." He zips up his jacket. "This is gonna be great." He punches me in the arm. "I'm really glad you're here."

"I hope you still feel that way when the season's over."

"Aw, c'mon, Coach. Why wouldn't I?"

I raise an eyebrow and sigh. "Usually I don't talk about stuff like this, but this one is definitely worth sharing."

"Go ahead."

"I was at a tournament one time in California, all boy wrestlers, no girls. In my last match, when the ref called us to the center of the mat to start, the boy I was wrestling rushed out of his corner like he was going to kill someone. The whole time there was this man, I guess it was his father, just pacing in his corner. Eventually, I lost 15 – 0, but he didn't pin me. That frustrated him, I guess. When I leaned over to shake his hand at the end of the match, he shoved me."

"He pushed you?" Coach Wagner asks.

"Almost all the way off the mat. The referee saw the whole thing, but he left the mat without doing anything about it."

Coach Wagner's eyes are as big as half-dollars.

"When I realized the ref was just going to brush me off, I ran back to the corner of the mat where the boy stood with his father. Neither of them would look at me."

"His father didn't even apologize to you?" Coach Wagner continues.

"The father was worse than his son. When I realized they were just going to ignore me, I ran in front of them, cutting off their path. At first, neither of them would say a word. They just glared at me. I just stood in front of them, demanding that they explain why they acted like that. Finally, the father held up a finger and pointed it at me and said, 'my son has nothing to say to you, Bitch. You got exactly what you deserve.'"

Coach Wagner shakes his head. "Well, look. I'm not going to lie to you, Lisa. Not everyone at Greenwood is totally on board with you being here, but in general, I think you'll find it friendlier than that. If someone's not treating you right here, I want to know about it. Deal?"

I consider the offer. "Deal."

The Colorado sun tucks itself in for the night. Thirty-two degrees of chill cause the tiny leaves on the bushes to brown and only the snow-tipped trees, still evergreen, remain somewhat as they had been last June when I was here for camp. Eventually, the curvy mountain path, barely wide enough for one vehicle, becomes a two-lane road as we slowly ascend the mountain from Greenwood to the suburb of Lakewood where Coach Dan Pierce lives. Coach Pierce's house will be my home for the season.

Coach Pierce lives alone, widowed four years ago after his wife lost a battle with diabetes and leukemia. He is a muscled, stocky shell of a former weightlifter now with an ample potbelly. He answers the door in a white undershirt and gray sweatpants, an outfit I imagine to be a uniform around his house. A large black Labrador retriever is a sloth by his side.

Coach Wagner introduces us and I am in unfamiliar territory all over again. Coach Pierce and I shake hands and exchange greetings, and I try to sound more at ease than I feel. Coach Pierce welcomes us into his home and offers us something to drink. The two coaches seem to be acquaintances more than friends, and I begin to wonder exactly what convincing has occurred to manage my living arrangement.

While the two of them catch up on the day's events, I pay attention to the dog, giving all of us something to focus on besides the awkwardness.

"That's Josh," Coach Pierce announces and pets the dog on his enormous furry face. "He's been around almost as long as this house, haven't ya Josh?" The dog gazes up at him and blinks.

"Hello, Josh," I bend down to see him face-to-face. "Hope you don't mind a little extra company around here."

"Oh, no," Coach Pierce says. "He'll like it. He gets a little lonely here anyway."

I wonder if we are still talking about Josh.

Coach Wagner stays another half an hour before announcing his departure. Then I am left alone in my new surroundings, which now seemed vast and foreboding. Coach Pierce shows me to the room where I will sleep, invites me to help myself to whatever might be lurking in the refrigerator, and then retires for the night.

Coach Pierce's door shuts and I am startled by aloneness. More than just the strange house and unfamiliar rooms, something feels final about the moment. My choice to move to Greenwood for the season is real now; there is no turning back. I tiptoe barefoot out to the kitchen to use the phone. Shadows from the moonlight sneak in through the skylights.

I dial my twin sister's phone number and chew on the inside of my lip as I wait for her to answer.

Historically, Laurel and I talked on the phone several times a week, usually every day. The relationship the two of us share kept us afloat through our parents' divorce and the storm that ensued afterward. More accurately, Laurel and I literally clung to each through it all. Almost every photograph taken from the time we aware of the other depicts us cheek to cheek, wrapped in each other's arms.

Laurel finally answers after four rings.

"It's just me and my suitcase full of wrestling gear," I whisper to her.

I share the information with her about living with Coach Pierce. "I thought I would be staying at Coach Wagner's house, but it looks like I'm at the football coach's house instead. He's got a great setup here: weight room in the basement and woods in the backyard. The only unfortunate thing is that I won't get paid until the end of the season, so I'm still not quite sure how I'm going to feed myself or pay for any of these phone calls I'm making."

"Didn't you plan any of that before you left?"

I remembered my Dad encouraging me to make arrangements, which I didn't do. "Not very well, I guess. But still, Coach

Wagner made it seem like that stuff was all worked out."

"How's it going besides that?"

"I took a close look around the room today at practice. Most of these guys are better wrestlers than I am. How I am supposed to teach them anything they don't already know? Especially when Coach Wagner announced to everyone that I was the national runner up last year at women's Nationals. I don't think he knows that only one other wrestler was in my weight class."

"Did you say anything?"

"What could I say?" I change the subject to avoid the discomfort. "Anyway, I won't be able to wrestle for about two more weeks because of the injury. That might give them a while to get used to me and for me to figure out what I'm going to do."

"How's your head?"

"It's healing. No more fluid dripping out of my ears or anything."

Laurel sighs. "Do you think this is worth it? Doing all of this for wrestling?"

The question startles me but I do not stammer. "It will be."

"I miss you," she says, ignoring my tough athlete routine.

I choke on my response and cough to cover up the threads of longing. "I miss you, too."

I slither back to my new room and shut the door. I consider calling Steve but wonder if he'll want to talk to me. Instead, I pull my knees to my chest and fall asleep in my clothes, comforting myself with a blanket of blind faith.

10

October 1991
Colorado

The door is unlocked when I come home after practice, a week since my arrival in Greenwood. Coach Pierce yells a greeting from his room. I shout back to him, hoping he will not come out to talk to me. But soon I hear his door open and a slow march down the carpeted hallway. When he appears, he holds a t.v. dinner in one hand and a fork in the other.

"Hey Big D." The emergence of the nickname surprises both of us. He comes over to the couch where I sit with the television turned on.

"A nickname? Does that mean you're starting to feel a little more comfortable here?"

I did not realize that my aloofness was noticeable. "It just takes me a while to figure my way around and get used to things."

"I understand," he says. "So you survived the first couple weeks of practice. How's it going?" he asks between bites of food.

I take a deep breath. "Besides the layoff, so far, so good."

"The guys treating you right?" he asks, without looking up.

I shrug. "Better than I expected actually."

Coach Pierce rises to set his empty tray on the kitchen counter. "Okay, c'mon. Cut it out." He smiles and cocks his head. "I've known some of those guys for too long to believe that everything's running that smoothly. What's going on?"

"Nothing! Everything's fine. I mean—there are a few guys that aren't taking to me too great, but other than that—really. It's fine. No big deal." I try to switch topics but Coach Pierce is far more interested in the first subject. After minutes of badgering and relentless questioning I give in. "Fine. You want a

70

name? Will that make you feel better? Nick Sway. Happy now?"

"No, not really. What about Nick? I thought you two were friends from camp."

"I don't think he would call us friends, necessarily. But we weren't enemies. I don't know what happened between then and now. He seems to enjoy insulting me in front of the wrestlers and he'd die before he took me seriously."

Coach Pierce perches on a kitchen stool. "Nick is probably just concerned about looking cool in front of his friends. Why don't you talk to him about it?"

I shoot a sarcastic glance in Coach Pierce's direction. "I'm sure that would go over well."

"I'll bet, if you actually sat him down and talked to him, you'd be surprised."

"Maybe," I say, chewing on the inside of my lip. "Can we stop talking about this?"

Coach Pierce puts his hands up in surrender. He ambles off to his bedroom again but I stay for a re-run of David Letterman. Reflections from the television flicker off of the living room walls. I stare at the phone sitting atop the kitchen counter just waiting to be picked up. Josh lies at the end of the couch; his head rests peacefully on the cushion. I scratch his ear with my foot and wonder what it would be like to be so content.

"What do you think, Josh? Should I call Steve?"

Josh's eyebrows move back and forth but his head remains motionless. I wanted to share the anticipation of my first day back on the mat with someone. No one was more fitting than the guy who was with me when I took the tumble.

I wander to the telephone and dial Steve's number. It rings four times, then five. The answering machine switches on.

"Hi, Steve, it's me. It's Lisa, calling from Colorado. Just wanted to let you know I'm here and to give you the number where I'm staying. Hope you're doing well." I hang up the receiver after leaving the phone number. Hearing his recorded voice pierces my heart and I feel the guilt of my yelling at him before I left. I close my eyes, angry with myself for the outburst.

What I visualize to be a triumphant return to the mat is overshadowed by an unexpected visit to the doctor. A hacking cough that I originally attribute to altitude sickness has not subsided and my throat is sore like I've been swallowing razor blades.

A plump nurse checks my temperature and my blood pressure, reviews my medical history, and then waddles away. I am alone in a curtained room hunching over on a paper-sheeted table waiting for the doctor. I hack and cough until I am too fatigued to sit up any longer and I flop backward onto the sterile pillow and fall asleep.

I awake to hear a melodious voice that belongs to the doctor. She pulls the curtain closed behind her and I come to attention, apologizing for falling asleep.

"That's okay, happens all the time," the doctor says, pulling a ballpoint pen from her coat pocket and scanning my chart. "Cribiform Plate fracture? When did that happen?"

I recount the wrestling story and consider that I have now lied to at least four medical professionals that I know of.

"So you're just barely healed from that, " she states matter-of-factly. "Any signs of drainage from the plate injury?"

"Not any more, " I promise, clearing my throat.

"Still wrestling?"

"Today was supposed to be my first day back. I've already taken ten weeks off."

"How long have you been coughing like that?" She sets my chart down on a nearby counter.

"A few weeks."

"You have a fever today. Have you been feverish over the last few weeks?"

"Maybe a little. Nothing major."

"What's not major?"

"A hundred maybe. I'm not sure."

"Today the nurse has you down for a hundred and two. That's not so good. Any other not-so-major symptoms you'd like to share with me?"

"My throat is killing me."

She puts her hands on my throat and presses.

"Could it be strep?" I squeak out.

"Have you had that before?"

"I get it every year."

"Open your mouth." She peers into my throat and comments on white spots all over my tonsils. "Looks like you've got it again. We'll do a throat culture to be sure, but I think you can count on it. It doesn't explain the coughing, though." She grasps her stethoscope and places the cold round plate on my back. "Take a deep breath."

I oblige, trying to get as much air as I can.

"Again." The wheezing is louder this time. "One more," she says, but I cannot do it without hacking. Pain from the cough starts deep and penetrates through my whole chest.

She pulls the stethoscope away and wraps it around her neck. Then she scribbles on my chart. "I can give you some antibiotics for the strep. You've got to rest for a few days to bring the fever down."

"What about the coughing?"

"That's a little trickier. Sounds like you have bronchitis. I can give you something for the cough, but those bronchial tubes will remain inflamed if you don't let them recover." I cough up some mucus. "I know you're not going to like this. But you really need to stay off the mat for another two weeks."

I shake my head emphatically and slide off the table to gather my belongings. "No way. I can't do it. I was already out for two months with this head thing and missed a huge tournament. I've got to get to Nationals in April." I hack some more.

The doctor puts a hand on my shoulder. "I would not insist on so much rest if it weren't for the head injury. You have to understand how serious that is. You're still risking a lot, Lisa. That fracture is just barely healed and your immune system is very taxed right now. By staying on the mat, you risk cracking the plate again. If you have strep when you do that, you're at risk for some very serious trouble."

We stare at each other. Finally I set my things back down, hoping she will believe that I have given in. "The bronchitis is going to kill my conditioning."

"I'm sure that's true, but you need the time off." She purses

her lips. "Sit tight. I'm going to chase down some antibiotics."
She vanishes.

I drop my head in my hands. Soon I overhear the doctor
speaking in hushed tones to one of the nurses.

"I don't know who's crazier, the guy in 4b who put his fist
through his living room window or the girl wrestler next to
him who thinks she's superwoman."

"I think they're both nuts," a nurse agrees.

"I think you're right."

When the doctor returns, I ignore the comments I heard
and accept the antibiotics. I need all the medicine I can get. I
am not taking any time off the mat.

In a few days I am able to swallow normally again. I have
finally returned to the wrestling mat, but I still cannot get
through practice without hacking like a smoker. Still, I join the
team for a run around the lake, the identical route as the one I
had torn through at camp. This time, I feel every rise in the
road and every twig beneath my feet. The pressure of the mountain air is wicked on my chest. I gulp oxygen through my mouth
but no amount is enough to ease the discomfort. I struggle to
make my way back to the wrestling room when I pass Nick
Sway. His fiery hair is matted against his head and sweat beads
from his pores.

"Good job, Nick," I say, barely getting the words out between my gasps for air. "Keep it up."

"Whatever," he says.

I think I misinterpret the tone at first. Then the confirma-
tion comes.

"Coach," he mocks.

The hostility startles me. I turn back to him, hoping for a
sign of playfulness. Instead, I only see the back of his shirt and
his figure disappearing down the dirt trail. The sting of disre-
spect nips at my heels the whole run back to the high school.

Before returning to the wrestling room, I stop in the restroom
to recover. Wiping perspiration from my forehead, I stare in
the mirror at my face, flushed from the blood rushing to cool

me. I pull several paper towels from the dispenser and blot my face, recounting Nick's tone. It bites me over and over. I crumple the wad of soiled towels and toss it into the wastebasket. I march out to the wrestling room, fueled by the bitterness swelling in my gut.

When all the wrestlers have completed the run, Coach Wagner rounds them up for practice. I shout after Nick.

"I want to talk to you for a second," I say, not certain if he will oblige. The other wrestlers taunt him, saying he is in trouble and harassing him. He rolls his eyes and follows me out to the hallway.

"Yeah?" He stands motionless with his hands on hips; sweat drips from his temples.

"I realize you may be uncomfortable with my coaching this team. I can't do anything about that except leave and I'm not going to do that. Since I've been here, you've been rude and insulting to me, and I'd like to know why."

He stares at me.

"Have I done something to offend you?" I press him for an answer. I am ready for a battle—some argument at least—but it never comes. He seems to be weighing the options.

"No, you haven't done anything to offend me."

"Well whatever it is, you better tell me. Otherwise, I have to conclude that you're scared to death of girls being in your wrestling room. And that alone would say a lot about you."

He stares at me, considering the ultimatum. Seconds seem like hours. "It's not you," he finally says, and puts his head down. "It's not you."

I am still expecting an argument, and his vulnerability surprises me. My heart races when I see him give in.

"What is it, then?" I demand.

Nick drifts over to the wall and slides down to sit against it. He hunches over for several minutes, shaking his head.

I join him against the wall. "Can you tell me?"

Tears form in the corners of his eyes. He tells a story that seems to have a life of its own, just waiting for someone to ask so that it could be disclosed, recognized, and paid attention to. "Ever since me and Troy were little, my dad talked about how we were gonna be great wrestlers. 'It's a tradition,' he says. His dad was a state champion, he was a state champion, and he expects me and Troy to be state champions, too. He built our whole family around wrestling. Wrestling is everything to him. It's…how he defines himself."

I recall camp last summer; how I assumed that his father's focus on scholarships and sponsorship was a blessing. Now I see how trapped Nick feels by all of it and how much must be riding on every match for him.

"When we're in public, he does weird things like point us out to his friends and shout, 'These are your next two state champions.' People pretend to be impressed by it, but deep down, I think they feel sorry for him."

"Ever since last year, when I didn't win State and Troy did, my Dad just wrote me off. Now he and all the coaches pay more attention to my brother than to me because he's a better wrestler than I am. It's always about Troy and his success. And since you got here, even you pay more attention to him. Coach Wagner does, too. Troy gets all the attention and I'm just Troy's older brother, the other one who wrestles. I'm so sick of it." He grits his teeth. "I'm so sick of it," he says again, holding his hands in fists and visible tears streaming down his face. "Dad never tells me I do anything right. He never notices anything I do. It's always Troy this and Troy that and isn't great what Troy did. No matter what I do, it's never enough." His words trail off and he drops his head again.

"Nick, I'm so sorry. I didn't—it wasn't meant—" I stumble over my words, feeling horrible for assuming the worst. "I didn't mean to bring all this up for you. Is there anything I can do?"

He sniffles and wipes his nose on his sleeve. "No. I just have to deal with it. I've always done that." He sniffles again. "Never mind." He gets up to leave. "Anything else?"

I stand up and face him. "Does your dad know how you feel?"

He shakes his head. "It wouldn't matter." He runs for the wrestling room, his final words still lingering in the air.

"You wrestle with Nick today," Coach Wagner says as we near the end of practice.

"Nick? Why?" I recognize this sounds like protest and I soften my tone. "I mean, why not one of the other guys I usually work out with?"

"Just thought you might want a different partner," Coach Wagner shrugs and walks away. The last thing I want is to get beat by a mediocre wrestler while the whole room watches. I was not supposed to get beat by most of them. I am the coach for crying out loud. I am too afraid of their reactions to my getting beat by a wrestler that half the others in the room can finish off, even if Nick did beat me at camp. On the other hand, I knew that if I did beat him, he would be devastated. Considering what Nick had just shared with me, I had to make another choice.

"I have another idea," I say, yelling after Coach Wagner. "How about Troy instead?"

Nick overhears the conversation and glares at me. He throws his wrestling gear on the mat and storms out of the room. No one goes after him and my heart breaks at not being able to tell him my true intentions. I am trying to protect both of us from our worst fears. I turn back to Coach Wagner.

"You sure you want that?" he asks.

"Positive."

Coach Wagner wrinkles his brow. "Okay, Coach. You're the boss." He saunters across the room and I watch as he asks Troy to wrestle me. He agrees and joins me in the corner of the room. When all partners are paired, Coach Wagner blows his whistle.

Troy and I lock up immediately. He slams my head into the mat with one forearm.

"Nice move," he whispers in my ear, and pulls my head into his chest.

"I didn't do anything yet," I growl and try to counter.

"I mean asking to wrestle me."

"What do you mean?" I square my hips off to him.

"Well, if I didn't know much about wrestling," he locks up harder on my head, "and I was trying to hide that from everybody," he cranks on my neck, "I would ask to wrestle the best guy in the room, too. That way, no one could tell how bad I was," he says, and throws me to my back. I lay dazed, less from the throw than from the dagger that he has spiked through my heart. I feel exposed and vulnerable, and I have obviously underestimated him. His brutality is a sharp contrast to Nick's sensitivity, and I try to remember that as I crawl back to my feet.

After practice, I arrive at the house and put the key in the front door lock. I drop my duffel bag in a corner and stretch out on the couch, my back aching and my calves sore. Coach Pierce appears shortly after.

"Hey, Little L," Coach Pierce announces as he sits down on a stool by the kitchen counter.

"Hey, Big D," I mumble.

He ambles over to the fridge and pours himself a glass of milk. "You don't sound so good," he says and gulps the water. "Did you go to the doctor yet?"

"Yeah, a week ago. I didn't care for her orders, though."

"Let me guess. The prescription included taking some time off but you're not, right?"

I hack up some mucus. "Right."

Coach Pierce rummages through the pantry. "And instead, you'll just pretend you're completely immune to it and hope it goes away, right?"

I do not answer that. Frankly, I am not in the mood to defend myself. "Did anyone call while I was gone?"

"Yeah, your sister called. And some guy named Steve."

I raise my head off the couch. "Steve called?" I am aware of my eagerness and try to disguise it.

"That's what he said. Do I get to know who he is?"

"Yeah, you can know. Just somebody from back home."

"A boyfriend maybe?"

"Maybe. I don't know if he would call himself that or not."

"Would you call him that?"

My face turns reddish. "Not yet. Someday maybe." I wait for Coach Pierce to leave the room so I can use the phone. He remains unmoved. I raise my eyebrows.

78

"Well?"

"Well what?" He says.

"Do you mind if I make a phone call?"

"Oh, you want privacy? Fine, Little L. I'm gone. But I would say that sounds like a boyfriend to me." He slowly leaves the room and I swear I hear him laughing to himself.

I move to the phone but pause before dialing. The butterflies in my stomach are not from being nervous for a change. They're from excitement at the prospect of talking with Steve. I think about Coach Pierce's suggestion that Steve and I are a couple, and the thought of us being together makes me smile.

Steve's phone rings twice before he answers.

"Hey, it's Lisa."

"Did you get my message?"

"Just that you called. I'm glad you did. How's everything going?"

"Okay. How's everything in Greenwood? The guys treating you okay?"

"That's the question of the day. The answer is yes, for now."

"How's your head?"

"It's pretty much healed. I got bronchitis and strep and was supposed to stop wrestling again, but I didn't."

"You didn't? Are you nuts?"

"Probably." This conversation reminds me of the last one. I remind myself to calm down. "Forget it. How's your season going?"

"Okay. We're up to three-a-day practices."

"Are you cutting any weight?"

"Nothing too severe. Ten pounds or so."

"That's not too bad."

"I guess not."

The conversation lulls. I think about him in his little house, curled up beneath a blanket. I picture myself next to him and contentment warms over me.

"This is funny."

"What's funny?" he asks.

"I haven't talked to you since I got here and we're both acting like that's no big deal." I remember my promise to myself. "What I really want to say is that I am sorry for yelling at you before I left. You didn't deserve it, and I really wish I hadn't acted like that."

Steve sighs. "That's okay. Let's just drop it."

"Deal," I agree.

"So when are you coming back?"

"The end of the season, I suppose. February probably, unless we go to State. We probably will, actually. We have a couple of good wrestlers."

"Selfishly, I hope you don't go."

His honesty startles me. I marvel at the security he has in himself to be so open, so trusting.

"Does that mean you want to see me when I come back?" I take a risk.

"Yeah, that's what it means."

"It's nice to be wanted."

"You are."

"Coach Pierce asked me—"

"Who's Coach Pierce?"

"The coach I'm staying with while I'm here."

"You live with a coach? Is he married?"

"No, he's widowed actually. Very sad story."

"Are you safe? I mean, is he like, hitting on you or anything?"

"For God's sake, Steve, no. He's more than twenty years older than I am."

"It's not unheard of."

"Can I just finish my thought please?" I smile to myself, enjoying this playful banter and imagining his brown eyes with a warm glow behind them.

"Go ahead."

"Thank you. Anyway, Coach Pierce asked me if you were my boyfriend."

"What did you say?"

"I said 'not yet.'" I can tell that he is smiling.

"Not yet, huh?"

"Should I have said something else?" I am hoping he tells me yes, that I should have said he was my boyfriend. He doesn't.

"Not if you didn't want to."

I sit down on the kitchen stool. His comment comes as a slight rejection and for a moment, I feel foolish. "You make me laugh."

"Why?" He asks.

"Because sometimes you don't give me a straight answer."

"That's because you're hard to read."

"What do you mean? I'm totally transparent."

Steve laughs out loud. "You are the most nontransparent girl I've ever met!"

"Is that a word? Nontransparent?"

"See what I mean? Don't change the subject."

"I'm not changing the subject! What do you mean I'm hard to read?" My curiosity is piqued, in spite of myself.

"I haven't known you very long, I admit that. But for the time we have spent together, I notice that you're pretty guarded."

"Guarded from what?"

"I have no idea. And I'll bet you won't tell me, either."

"I would if I knew what you were talking about." I know what he means, but admitting that is revealing in itself.

"For example, I don't know anyone else who would try so hard to beat me at a wrestling match in my own house and break her nose and skull doing it."

My heart pounds. "How does that make me guarded?"

"Come on, Lisa. Anyone with that much at stake has something to lose. You're just not going to tell anyone what it is."

Steve is right. I remember the wrestling match at his house, how important it was to me to prove to him, to me, that I was so tough and wouldn't give up. The price I paid for it was ten weeks off the mat, and I don't feel any more secure than I did before breaking my nose and my skull. I just feel foolish and guilty for lying to everyone about it.

"Are you still there?" Steve asks. "Lisa?"

"Yeah, I'm here. What do you want me to say?"

"Nothing, I was just—I'm just trying to point something out to you."

"Okay, well, thank you. Can we talk about something else now?"

"Sure, let's talk about something else."

My thoughts are disordered and jumbled now and I find nothing else to say. "Actually, I guess I'm pretty tired. I just called to tell you I'm sorry. Maybe we can talk later?"

"Are you mad now?"

"No. I'm just tired. Can I call you this weekend?"

"That would be great. Thanks for calling back."

"No problem."

"And Lisa?"

"Yeah?"

"If you wanted to call me your boyfriend, that would be okay."

A smile starts, but something makes me reject him. "I'll call you next week, okay?"

He sighs. "Bye."

"Bye, Steve."

I hang up the phone.

I think about Steve's assessment of me: guarded and scared of losing something, whatever it is. I lumber back over to the couch and lay down, thoughts of Steve's words hovering in my mind. The phone ringing startles me.

"It's me," Laurel said. "Did I wake you up?"

"No. Are you okay?"

"I just miss you. How's your head? Are you wrestling again?"

I do not say anything about the strep and bronchitis. "Yeah, I'm wrestling again. Not particularly well, but whatever."

"I don't like that you hurt yourself wrestling. I mean, this time your head healed, but something really bad could have happened to you."

Laurel has this way of forcing me to acknowledge that I'm not invincible, mostly just because she's not shaken by her own vulnerability. She's not afraid to be afraid. It actually seems to make her stronger.

"I have to tell you something, but you have to promise not to tell anyone."

"What is it?"

"Promise not to tell anyone?"

"Okay, I promise. What is it? Are you okay?"

I relate the story about wrestling Steve, including all the details. "The ladder fell right on the bridge of my nose."

"Oh my God."

"I was too embarrassed to tell people that I got so caught up in that silly wrestling match, so I made up the wrestling practice story."

"Not to mention the fact that you scared your entire family."

I can tell she is angry, and I do not blame her, but I am determined to tell her the whole story. If I am going to confess, I'm going to do it right. "It gets worse. I did a press interview the other day and they asked me if I had ever been injured while wrestling. The newspapers just ate up the fact that I had this life-threatening head injury sustained during practice. Everyone reacted like I was this brave wrestler, totally invulnerable and invincible. The part I can't figure out is why that felt so good."

"This is insane."

"I know it is. But for the first time, I've got people inviting me to their wrestling rooms, their wrestling camps, and their interviews. If the image that's created by my surviving a head injury makes them feel better about those invitations, I'm sure as hell not going to deny anyone that, including me."

Laurel is silent.

"I'm sorry. I don't mean to raise my voice. I'm just—I have a lot going on right now." I seem to be apologizing a lot lately.

"I can see that. I also know that you hardly ever rely on anyone else for help in situations where you need it."

Her insight silences me. She is so right. To me, asking for help always means some kind of weakness, some sort of vulnerability. It's like the definitive X on Dr. Connor's symptom sheet.

"Laurel, you're probably right about that. But right now, I just need you to promise me you won't say anything about how the injury happened."

After several moments, she responds. "Fine. I won't say anything. But just for the record, I don't think you're taking very good care of yourself."

I sigh, wondering if she's right.

11

December 1991
Colorado

The whoops and hollers of our winning wrestling team and its fans sound farther away than they are as I sit in the boys' locker room awaiting Coach Wagner. We beat our rivals by one match tonight and it is our standard practice to anecdotally review our wrestlers' performance immediately after a meet.

I lean on a fixed bench and stretch my legs, revealing my discomfort in the skirt I've chosen to wear. Coach Wagner prefers not to wear ties, but he usually wears a sport coat. I figure I can branch out, too, in support of his effort. He arrives minutes later, smile pasted to his face and ready to high five me.

"Not bad for a midseason meet." He slaps my hand.

"Not bad at all," I say, and reciprocate the hand slap.

"I think we're well on our way to a great District showing."

"Barring any unforeseen disasters, which we will not entertain, I think you're right," I agree.

Coach Wagner studies me. "You seem a little down, Coach. What's the matter?"

I sigh and consider the options, but it will do no good to hide it from him. "I probably should have just erased it before you came in." I approach the blackboard and turn it around on its wheels. "But I made you a deal." Chalked darkly in large block letters is a message.

I WANT TO SCREW GREENWOOD'S ASSISTANT COACH.

Coach Wagner reads it and shakes his head. "Oh man, Coach. I'm sorry. I don't know what to say."

We both move for the chalk eraser at the same time.

"Please," he says, "it's the least I can do." He slides the

eraser across the chalked letters. The two of us sit side by side on the thin metal bench like crows on a wire. Had I wings, I would have spread them and flown away, high into the Greenwood snow-tipped peaks.

"Must have happened when they were in here changing before the meet," Coach offers.

My eyes are glassy and my shoulders hunched. "Yeah, I guess so."

"I'll let their coach know about it. We'll make sure it doesn't happen again."

I shake my head. "Please don't say anything. It's enough having to show you."

He protests. "I'm not going to have visiting teams coming in insulting my coaching staff."

I shrug. "Whatever." I surprise myself with my lack of vengeance. It is less maturity than apathy, but it takes energy to be angry, and I cannot afford to expend any more.

We sit for a moment. "Can I buy you dinner?" he asks.

"I'm starving." I stand up with resolution. "One favor, though."

"Name it."

"I have got to get into some sweat pants. This skirt is driving me crazy."

He chuckles. "I'm not enjoying my suit very much, either." He lumbers through the locker room door. "Meet you outside."

I cannot help wondering which one of the visiting wrestlers had written the message. *I wonder if I wished him good luck before his match. Did he shake my hand after the meet?* The chalkboard stands before me, the message erased but the questions still etched in my mind.

12

February 1992
Colorado

"Where are you headed?" Coach Pierce asks me as I pack clothes into a duffel bag.

"Greenwood's wrestling in the state tournament."

"State wrestling already?" He crosses his arms and leans in the doorway. "Boy, that came fast."

"I know it." I roll socks in a ball and throw them in the bag.

"Are you still going to women's Nationals in April?"

"Of course I am." I scowl. "Why would you think I'm not?"

"Just curious."

I throw my last T-shirt into my bag. "I'm surprised you didn't know the answer."

I feel Coach Pierce's stare. "I don't know. Coach Wagner mentioned something about you needing to work harder in the wrestling room."

The words stun me. I stop packing and glare at him. "Did he really say that?"

He does not answer the question. "Come with me," he says instead.

"Did he really say that?" I ask again.

"Come on, Little L. Just for a second."

I zip my bag. "Where am I going?"

"You're so stubborn. Just be quiet and come here." He walks out to the full-length mirror at the end of the hallway. He gently nudges me in front of him and stands with both hands on my shoulders. He looks over me into the mirror.

"What's supposed to happen?" I resent his attempt at control, however harmless.

"What do you see when you look in the mirror?"

"What do you mean?" I glare at him and shrug. "I see what you see."

He crosses his arms in front of him. "Do you like what you see?"

The question is loaded and I resent it. I cannot think of a graceful way out of it. Even if I say yes, the mere fact that his asking me indicates that he sees something, or the absence of something, that prompts him to ask the question. I do not need him digging around my ego. But he has asked it, and I am forced for a split second to think about it.

"Of course I like what I see." My throat is tight and my heartbeat rages.

"Do you, really?"

"Yes, I do, really." Now I cross my arms.

"Honestly?"

"Yes."

"You sure?"

"What kind of game is this?" I uncross my arms and lean against the wall. "I already said yes."

"I'm not trying to make you uncomfortable," he says, placing a hand on my shoulder again.

I want to toss him into the closet and lock it. Instead, I pretend to listen, all the while looking straight through him.

"I just want you to be honest with yourself."

"What makes you think I'm not honest with myself?"

He shrugs. "You tell me."

"Nothing personal, but I don't need to defend myself to you or to anybody else." I turn when a honk sounds in the driveway. Coach Wagner is on time as usual and I am grateful for it. "I have to go, Coach." The defiance in my voice is clear. "Thanks for the talk," I say.

I mockingly placed my hand on his shoulder, patting him a couple times. I grab my packed bag and run out the door.

13

February 1992
Colorado

Sprinkling snow dots the crisp winter air and engulfs Denver, Colorado, the venue for the State High School Wrestling tournament. Three of our wrestlers have qualified for the tournament: Troy Sway at 103 pounds, Chris Lannum at 171 pounds, and our heavyweight, Matthew Downs. For the second year in a row, Nick Sway does not qualify, a situation to which he is sadly accustomed and one that causes significant discomfort in his household, I am certain.

Coach Wagner and I ride together in the van and lead a convoy of the competing wrestlers and their parents to the hotel where reservations await us. We arrive in Denver in the late afternoon with much time to spare before the first session. We all agree to meet at the stadium at five o'clock for weigh-ins and then huddle prior to the first round. In the meantime, I lay in my hotel bed staring at the ceiling and relive the disturbing conversation I had with Coach Pierce before I left. My blood boils as I recount his face, and I wonder whether Coach Wagner actually made the comment about my not working hard enough in the wrestling room. The pit in my stomach forces me to wonder what it all means.

Just before five o'clock, I head out across the hotel parking lot and make my way to the stadium. The Denver wind taunts me as I dodge among the hundreds of parked cars and buses. My head whirls in the drama and tension, as irresistible to me now as it had been so many years ago when I used to watch the tournaments in Cedar Falls. The intensity is no different as I pull open the massive metal doors that reveal the venue. White wrestling mats lay about, paired with high tech digital scoring pyramids and black- and white-striped uniformed referees. Bright spotlights hang from metal beams atop the stadium. I head to the first entryway I spot and jog down the smooth concrete stairs to the section where we agreed to meet.

Team Greenwood is already settled into the bleachers with coolers, blankets, and duffel bags. Our three athletes who will be wrestling are among the hundreds of others reviewing the 16-wrestler brackets on the far wall. The other wrestlers who have come along for support are wound up like battery powered toys, running across sections of bleachers, pointing out attractive girls, and causing general commotion.

I locate Coach Wagner who is slurping on a soft drink. I scoot past a few wrestlers to greet him.

"Weigh-ins go okay?" I ask.

"No problems at all."

"What's their mood?"

Coach Wagner shrugs. "Matthew seemed pretty relaxed, but he doesn't wrestle until tomorrow. Troy and Chris, I don't really know. Can't really tell. Maybe you can get a temperature from them."

"That I can do."

Coach Wagner gazes out at the mats. "I need to talk to you about Troy's match tonight."

"It's gonna be good."

"That's for sure, that's for sure," Coach Wagner agrees.

He seems to be hesitating. "Is everything okay?" I ask, just to be sure.

Coach Wagner takes a deep breath. "Troy's father talked to me earlier. He'd really like to be on the mat for his son's match." He slurps his drink again.

"That's fine. We can just drag another chair over for him."

Coach Wagner avoids my eyes. "Actually, the tournament rules only allow two coaches in the corner," he says. He sets his empty drink cup down and folds his arms in front of his chest.

I finally understand what he is trying to say. "You're not serious. You're not asking me to sit up here and watch."

Coach Wagner says nothing and squirms in his seat.

"You aren't serious, are you?" I repeat.

"Coach, I'm sorry," he concedes. "I didn't know what else to say to him. He's really invested in his son's wrestling."

"He's invested? I'm the one who gets beat up by him every day. Half the wrestlers in the room won't touch him."

"I know, I know," he places an open palm up to quiet me. "But we've always made kind of a special allowance for Troy's father. He sponsors the little kids' summer wrestling program and he gives a lot of money at the booster club meetings—"

"Really? How much is my matside seat costing these days?"

Coach Wagner pulls his straw out of his empty soda cup and chews on it. "Lisa, I'm not saying it's right."

I know he has made his decision. I cannot help but wonder if this is his way of conveying his disapproval. Maybe he really did tell Coach Pierce I wasn't working hard enough. Either way, I wish he'd come out and say it.

Gradually, the stadium fills with more spectators, wrestlers, and floor workers. Greenwood's fan club is growing, too, as several sets of parents and more relatives join to watch the excitement. The commotion continues in the bleachers as the announcer instructs all 171-pound wrestlers to be prepared in the next half hour for their bouts. Finally, Chris Lannum is due to wrestle.

I had a certain fondness for Chris from the first day I met him, though I could not put my finger on why exactly. Behind his confidence and boyish demeanor, something exists that attracts me to him, a quality I suspect I do not possess. I always found myself listening a little more closely to him than to the others, watching his matches more often, and wondering what it is behind that cocky smile that intrigues me so much.

When the announcer's call booms again, Chris rises from his seat to obey the orders when the woman sitting next to him tugs on his arm. "Give 'em hell, sweetie." She kisses his cheek. "I'll be here watching for you." She looks both proud and ambivalent about his going off to war. I perceive she has attended many of his matches, though, judging from her timely words of encouragement and the sense not to push for a response when Chris trots off without a thank you. She sits back down in her seat.

"I'm guessing you're Chris's mother?" I ask, holding out an open hand. She turns to me and returns the handshake.

"I am proudly that." Her face glows.

I introduce myself as the assistant coach, a statement that was usually a conversation stopper or starter depending on the personality and mood of the other.

"I've heard about you," she says, and winks.

"And I about you," I say and release her hand as I stand to my feet. "Your son told me that you'd be coming. He's glad to have you here." Satisfaction lights up her face. I wonder what history exists between the two of them. Maybe they have been close since he was young, or maybe they have been through the worst and are coming out the other side. Either way, I knew something of the need to be wanted.

Chris wins his first match handily, and I am proud to be sitting in the coach's corner for it. Coach Wagner jumps up in excitement and we congratulate each other, thrilled that Chris has come through this way in his senior year. The celebration continues in the stands as his mom throws her arms around him and he accepts.

For Troy's matches, I grant Coach Wagner's wishes and watch from the stands. I'm sure I wear a cynical expression as Troy's father drops into the empty chair in the corner. While I have no illusions that my presence mat side will impact Troy's ability to wrestle through any tight situations, I feel as certain that his father's presence is detrimental given the pressure he puts on his son. I toy with this thought for a while, and it distracts me from feeling dismissed by Coach Wagner whom I counted on to make a different choice.

When the sun sets over Denver, team Greenwood has posted six wins. Chris and Matthew each win their two matches with relatively little effort. Troy wrestles in overtime to win his second match of the day. The worst our wrestlers can place individually is sixth, making this a success regardless of what happens the rest of the tournament.

Back at the hotel, I see Chris and shout for his attention. He carries a full bucket of ice from the machine and wears only gym shorts. His face is slightly pale and circles are forming beneath his eyes.

"Congratulations, champ," I say. "Excellent job today."

"Thanks. I was nervous."

It occurs to me that he probably has no idea what nervousness really feels like. "Didn't show it."

Chris swirls the ice bucket and smiles at me.

"Did I catch you on the way to sleep?"

"Nah, I'm too restless. I was just getting some ice for my mom." He sets the bucket down on the carpet.

"I met her today. She seems really happy to be here."

"I know it."' He folds his arms and leans against the wall. Finally the silence becomes awkward.

"Well, it's late, I'm sure you're tired."

"Yeah," he agrees. "I better go. Got a big match in the morning." He starts for the door.

"Chris?" I stop him, not certain what I want to ask. The words do not come and I say instead, "You're gonna do great tomorrow."

He looks at me and nods his head. "Hope so," he says, and slips away.

The next morning, Coach Wagner joins me in the restaurant for breakfast before our ritual march to the stadium. He has conducted some research on our opponents and gives me the rundown.

"Big day today. The 103-pounder from Cherry Creek is a hammer. Troy is in for a good match."

I sip the last of my black decaf. "Think he can win it?"

"Troy or the Cherry Creek kid?"

I smirk. "You're worried Troy can't beat him."

"Troy is a great wrestler."

"No doubt about it," I say. "That's not what I asked you."

"Ask me something else." He thumbs through his wallet for cash.

"Do I have to sit in the stands again for his match?"

The waitress brings our check. "I don't think he'll win it," he said, answering both of my questions at the same time.

Team Greenwood marches across the parking lot in preparation for the second day of competition. In the stadium, vendors peddle T-shirts, wrestling shoes, and instructional videos. Cheerleaders dress in spirited garb and prance through the corridors trying to keep up with their wrestlers. Parents and coaches follow every move of their sons' matches on video cameras and scream encouragement from the stands. I manage to find my way to our camp of parents and wrestlers. Chris's mother fidgets in her seat while she awaits his next match. I sit behind them, looking down over the tops of their worried heads at the mats below.

"Coach," Chris sneaks up behind me and taps my shoulder. His eyes have a scarlet tint and his face is flushed. He smiles that cocky smirk anyway, but an unusual sensitivity is beneath it. "I don't feel very good. "

I turn toward him. "What's the matter?"

"I don't know." His voice quivers. I signal for him to follow me up the stairs and out of the way of the other wrestlers. He runs behind me as we find a corner safely away from the crowd.

"Tell me what's up," I continue.

"I can't focus on anything and my heart is racing. I could hardly sleep last night at all." He stares into me, searching for an answer. "This morning I woke up and my stomach was in a knot. My fingers and toes are like icicles. My muscles are all tight and I can't seem to concentrate. I feel like I'm going crazy." Chris pulls a hand from his pocket to clear the hair from his face and I notice his hand shaking. He exhales deeply. "What am I gonna do?"

My heart sinks deep into my chest. I am unsure who feels more exposed. I stand poised for what seems like several minutes, searching for the right balance of advice and self-preservation. I swallow hard and hope Chris does not see the sweat beading on my forehead. His words hang in the air, taunting me. I chew on the inside of my lip, and we both wait for me to find something to say.

"You're just a little nervous, that's all," I say. "Try to take some deep breaths, and relax. You're gonna be okay," I say.

He looks through me, innocent eyes searching for something to take it all away.

Coach Wagner finds us at the stairway landing. "Hey, we gotta go." His command is pressured. "You ready, buddy?"

Chris faces me and exhales loudly. The two of them race down the stairs. For the first time, I realize the quality absent within myself that makes Chris's manner so appealing. He is vulnerable, and he is wholly secure in it.

Chris gets caught in more cradles and headlocks than I have ever seen in one match. Coach Wagner and I are all over the sidelines, screaming with advice and support until our throats are raw. I cringe at every pinning combination, thinking each one will be the end of the match for Chris. At the end of each period he glances at us with his hands up, looking for direction and advice. He tries everything we suggest, even some unorthodox moves, but nothing can overcome the skill and experience of his opponent.

At the conclusion of the match, the referee holds the hand of the other wrestler high in victory. Chris ambles off and collapses on the floor, his chest heaving and his skin scarlet with blood at the surface. He lay motionless on his back on the cold floor with his hands over his face.

Losses like these in the semi-final rounds were the beginning of a downward spiral for us. For Troy particularly, the tournament ended with a loss to a wrestler he had beaten before. I watch passively as Troy's father stands over him throwing pressured, wild gestures. Troy does not move, the tears streaming off his flushed cheeks, dripping onto the cement floor.

The following morning, Coach Wagner and I sit in the parking lot of the hotel, car running, waiting to lead the convoy back home.

Lisa Whitsett

"Sorry this year didn't turn out quite the way you wanted it, Coach."

"Ah, come on. We won Districts, didn't we? And we took three to State and they all placed. Can't ask for a lot more than that."

"Except maybe three state champions."

"Well, yeah. Except that." Coach Wagner reaches into a brown paper bag in the back seat. "I was saving this for the banquet next week, but you look like you could use it now." He hands me a plaque, a deep blue colored face mounted on dark wood. It is heavy and meaningful in my hands.

I read out loud. "Thank You to Lisa Whitsett, the Nation's First Female Wrestling Coach." Seeing my name plainly on the very final, conclusive piece of hardware chokes me. "Thanks, Coach." I hug him.

"You coming back next year?"

I look at him and half smile. He knows the answer.

"I can't really blame you." He pours some coffee from a thermos. "Well, if nothing else, you certainly made a name for yourself here."

"Meaning?"

"Some local radio station does daily sports trivia and the question yesterday was, 'What is the name of the female wrestling coach in Colorado?' One of the wrestlers' parents told me that."

"No kidding?"

"No kidding," he says. "And partly because of you, Colorado is lifting the ban on females wrestling in the state."

I chuckle at that thought. "I can't believe people let them write a law like that anyway."

"I know it. We're pretty backwards here sometimes."

I did not agree with him out loud, but I think it.

"Coach?" I start. "Did you tell Coach Pierce I wasn't working hard enough?"

He sips his coffee. "Yeah. I did."

My heart pounds, but I say nothing.

"Don't you want to know why?" he nudges.

I shrug. "Do you want me to know why?" I stare at him.

He squares off to face me. "Lisa, I've seen you wrestle a thousand times in the room, right?"

I nod.

"Recovering from a head injury, during bronchitis, strep throat. Doesn't matter. You wrestle right through it, right?"

"So?"

"So, why don't you wrestle like that at tournaments?"

His words hang in the air, biting like the chill of Colorado winter.

Coach Pierce is in bed already when I return home. The house is dark except for the hallway light that shines over the full-length mirror. I wander over and stand before it, recalling my conversations with Coach Wagner and Coach Pierce. Their words creep in like an eerie fog.

14

March 1992
Cedar Falls, Iowa

"Welcome back," Dr. Connor greets me with a smile and a handshake when I return to her office in early March.

"It's good to be back," I say and look around her office. "You've done some remodeling, I see." She has added two bookshelves to one of the walls.

"Needed more room for this year's research projects. The filing cabinet and my desk just weren't enough." She gestures to a new chair. "And your new seat awaits."

My face lights up. A leather chair has replaced her old one. "Very nice," I caress the arms of the chair, sit down in it and get comfortable. When we are both settled, I look across the desk at her. "It's been an interesting few months," I suggest.

"I can imagine. How's your skull?"

"Healed, as far as I can tell. No more leaking fluid—that stopped back in late November. I got back on the mat right after that."

"How was that?"

"Painful. But you do what you got to do, right?"

"I suppose so. How do you feel now?"

"Out of shape. Slow, sluggish. Not ready for Nationals. I was so concerned with making sure everyone thought I was a good coach. I don't even think I was."

"Why would you say that?"

"I wasn't ready to the lead that team. They needed someone with more experience. I think they deserved better." I shake my head.

We sit silently for a moment. Then Dr. Connor asks, "What would you like to talk about today?"

"Can I tell you my plan for Nationals?"

"Sure."

"I've decided to cut weight from 105 pounds to ninety-seven pounds."

Her eyes widen. "You're cutting eight pounds? That's a lot of weight off of you, isn't it?"

"I don't want to get accustomed to being second. I figure the best way to avoid falling into that trap is to start over in a new weight class."

She contemplates the information. "How long do you have to cut the weight?"

"Nine weeks; that's about a pound a week."

She says nothing.

"Wrestling up a weight to 110 would be ridiculous," I continue. "Our world silver medallist, Shannon Williams, cuts hard to make that weight and she is still strong after cutting. The only answer is the eight pounds."

I expect her to nod in agreement with my logic and forethought. Instead, she stares at me from across her desk.

"So what do you think?" I ask, with a pressured tone.

"I think it will hinder your performance," she states.

I ignore her comment. "Psychologically, I'm not ready to walk into that tournament and win the national championship if I have to wrestle 103 pounds again. It's like a curse or something. I figure if I just start over, it might give me the edge I need to get it together for once and wrestle like I know I'm capable of wrestling. It can't hurt."

"It might hurt."

"I'm willing to risk it." I am startled by her disapproval. I want her to say this is a good idea to instill some confidence in me that this last ditch effort might work.

Instead, she sighs deeply. "What about the techniques we talked about? The triggers?"

I look down at my feet. "I'll keep working on it."

"I don't think this is a good idea, this weight cutting situation. You should really be tapering off and resting a few days before your tournament, not cutting weight. It's probably the worst thing for you."

"Worse than losing the national championship again?"

She sits for a moment before rising to her feet and walking me to the door. "Let me know how it goes," she says.

I start to say I will but she shuts the door. I stand idle for a moment, hurt by her reaction. The disapproval still stings as I hoist my backpack over both shoulders and lumber down the hallway.

"Hold on, I'm on my way," Steve yells from the upstairs of his two-story house. I had knocked loudly several times on the sturdy wooden door, hoping for a response. He swings it open wide and appears momentarily shocked.

"You're back."

"I am that." He stares at me for a moment and then comes to me, wraps his arms around my waist and smothers me with a warm embrace. "I am so happy to see you," he whispers in my ear.

I release the breath I am holding, relieved that our verbal pact we had made on the phone still held true. "You cannot imagine how glad I am to be back." I whisper to him. We pull back from each other. "And to see you."

He smiles and invites me inside, holding my hand the whole time.

"Looks like you're almost done with the house." I notice.

"Just about," he says and pulls out a chair for me. "A few more coats of paint upstairs and it should be good as new." We smile at each other and then laugh like school children.

"Okay, I'll go first," he says. "I really missed you a lot."

"I missed you, too."

"Having you away was really miserable."

"To say the least," I agree. "It was really hard to be away from my boyfriend that long."

He stares at me, his soft brown eyes glowing with life behind them. "I didn't enjoy having my girlfriend gone that long either."

He caresses my hand. "So it is official? We're doing the boyfriend and girlfriend thing?"

"Let's try it."

He smiles a warm and gentle grin. "Should we start by

having dinner tonight?"

"Sounds good," I agree. "There's one catch. I can't eat any-thing."

He grimaces. "We're going to dinner but we're not eating?"

"*I'm* not eating," I clarify. "I have eight pounds to lose."

"Nationals?"

"Coming up fast," I confirm.

"Not the beginning to our relationship I had hoped for, but I'll take it."

15

April 1992
Las Vegas, Nevada
National Freestyle Wrestling Tournament

My plane lands in Las Vegas in early afternoon. By the time I get to the hotel, it is five o'clock in the evening. I have cut weight for the last eight weeks prior to Nationals, and I am confident I have only a pound to lose, if that.

I strip all my clothes off in my hotel room and beneath it all, my skin is drier than I anticipate. Steve had reluctantly lent me his plastic exercise suit, which I wore on the plane, but even that has not pulled as much water from my body as I expected. I change into dry sweats and a sweatshirt and find my way back downstairs to the on-site fitness center where I locate a digital scale. I disrobe, step onto the black pad, and watch as the red numbers bounce between 103 and 104 pounds. *Oh my God.* My heart thumps in my chest and my breath quickens. *This cannot be right.* I back off of the scale and step on again to make certain. The scale shows 103 pounds. I have six pounds of water to shed in two hours.

I race back up the stairs to my room and grab every piece of clothing I brought: a pair of shorts, two T-shirts, three pairs of sweat pants, three sweatshirts, four pairs of socks, and another pair of plastics. My lucky stocking cap, without which I never cut weight, tops off the outfit. I race back down to the fitness center in less than ten minutes.

I pull my hood over my head and peddle furiously on a stationary bike. I wipe my mouth, drier with each rotation of the pedals. *When I left my house this morning I thought I was on—97 pounds. I get off the plane and I'm six over.* I am determined to lose the water if it kills me. Nothing is keeping me out of the 97 pound class.

Forty-five minutes later I am fiery from the heat and have

closed my eyes. Still on the stationary bike, I rest my forehead on the handlebars and will the water to come off. My skin burns from the excessive heat and my chest ignites with a fiery sensation. The minutes tick off like days. I mumble with the rhythm of the peddling. *Keep going. A little bit more. Keep going.* Meanwhile my tennis shoes soak with sweat.

After fifteen minutes, I meander to the scale again. I strip to my shorts and T-shirt and step on the scale: 102 pounds. I stumble more than step off the scale; my body is limp and depleted. I am glassy-eyed now as I wander toward the revolving hotel door, thus far keeping me safe from the blistering heat of Las Vegas. I push on the door as it sucks the air through and thrusts me into hell. Waves of torturous heat hover on the asphalt as I set out to cut the final five pounds off my exhausted body.

My feet are cement blocks as I complete the first mile of a jog. My lips and tongue form the familiar white paste along their sides from thirst and the sweat that had started dripping off my forehead stops completely. I chant to myself amidst the heat waves rising off the asphalt. *This is where is gets tough, Lisa. Your mind will give out before your body will. Don't let a few pounds stand in the way of your national championship. Just keep moving. The pain is temporary.*

By the second mile, my vision blurs and the dizziness engulfs me. I pause for a moment to regain my balance and my knees buckle. The fall startles me and shoots adrenaline through my body, just enough to give me the energy to get back up. I get to my feet but I can hardly breathe. My chest is like fireworks exploding. The Las Vegas sun blankets me; I am being cremated as I push ahead, praying for the water to come off. I wipe my forehead but only minimal sweat seeps through my pores. The pavement is blistering but my skin turns clammy and cold. I am disconnected from the experience somehow, crying simply because I have nothing else to do. Tears stream down my cheeks and I mutter to myself to put one foot in front of the other, hoping it is enough, but knowing it never is.

I finally reach the hotel in a haze of delirium and halluci-
nation. I have lost track of where I am, what time it is, where I
am going. I run more laps around the hotel as other guests
stare at me. I promise myself that I will complete one more lap
around the hotel when I feel a burning sensation in the left
part of my chest so strong I think my heart has exploded. The
pain sends me collapsing to the ground. I hear it pounding
through all the layers. Heat exhaustion or heat stroke, either
way it didn't matter now. I lay in a heap beneath the scorching
sun, the asphalt burning my skin. I am too exhausted to get
up, even though my mind is telling me to get back to my feet.
My body is done. So is my attempt to make the 97-pound weight
class.

For what it's worth, I stick to my plan not to wrestle 103
pounds, and wrestle in the 110-pound weight class. Feeble at
100 pounds, I meet Shannon Williams, solid and strong at 110
pounds, in our first match the next day. When the whistle
sounds, she blows through me with a double leg takedown. I
fall backwards and hit the back of my head on the mat. I remember almost nothing about the match after that except her
hand being raised in victory. When I leave the mat, I wobble
over to a corner and slide down against the wall. Dazed and
confused, I glance around the venue. I have no memory of
why I am there. I see the wrestlers, and push to my feet, thinking that I am supposed to get up and wrestle. But I look down;
I am already wearing my wrestling gear and it is damp with
sweat. I see the 125-pound wrestlers in action and I realize
that I have already wrestled. I have no memory of it; Shannon
hit me so hard that it knocked me out. I remember nothing
from the time I stepped on the mat until this moment.

The on-site trainer confirms that I have a slight concussion,
but she gives me my choice to wrestle or not. The thought of
living with myself after declining to wrestle makes the choice
obvious, even if it is Shannon I have to wrestle again. So that
night I lay in bed, concussed head pounding and stomach ach-

ing. I have so dehydrated myself that no amount of fluid heals me. I am parched and ravenous, but I cannot keep anything down without throwing up. Fleeting self-respect does not change the inevitable. I have lost my second national championship.

16

May 1992
Cedar Falls, Iowa

"You were right," I say to Dr. Connor. "Nationals were a disaster."

"What happened?"

"I cut too much weight. I was too weak to stand, got knocked out cold and walked away with second place by default."

"What do you mean default?"

"Only two of us showed up to contest the weight class."

"I see," she says. "Well, if nothing else, you've prompted me to add another symptom to the list."

"What's that?"

"Insanity," she says.

I am not sure she's kidding. "That's fair."

She studies me. "You can't help it, can you?"

"What?"

"Feeling good about the weight cutting. About torturing yourself."

"What do you mean?"

"If wrestling were not enough to prove to the world that you're made of steel, wrestling after days of dehydration and food deprivation certainly will."

"I don't know what you want me to say to that."

"I'm just suggesting that you be honest with yourself."

"You're not the first."

"What?"

"Never mind. I don't cut weight to prove anything to anyone. I cut weight so I can wrestle the weight I need to in order to have the best chance of winning."

"Says you. Just for the record? The experience I've had with wrestlers leads me to believe that weight cutting is about a lot more than wrestling at a particular weight. It has to be; I don't think you would do it to yourselves otherwise. It's part of the whole mentality—the toughness, the invulnerability. Do you have any idea how harmful cutting weight is for your body?"

"I do now." We sit silently for a moment. "Could we talk about my next tournament?"

She twirls a pencil between her fingers, studying me again. "When is it?"

"November fourth. If I place high enough, I get to wrestle in a tournament in Europe. If I wrestle well there, I might be able to make up for not winning Nationals."

"So," she glances through a calendar. "That's six months from now. Are you willing to try a few things we haven't done before?"

"Anything. You name it."

"First, don't cut anymore weight."

"No problem. I'm cured of it. I'm wrestling at 103 again from now on."

"Second, go see a nutritionist. You look like hell."

"Thanks."

"Lastly, let's talk about your training regimen. How many times a week do you practice?"

"I wrestle Monday through Friday and sometimes Saturdays if I can find a partner to meet me on his own time."

"What else?"

" I run three miles three times a week in the mornings."

"What else?"

"I lift weights four times a week."

"Anything else?"

"I run the dome stairs a lot with my Dad."

"So, all together, you train almost every day of the week and you train sometimes as much as four times a day."

"Right."

"When do you rest?"

"What do you mean?"

Dr. Connor laughs. "I mean, when do you stop moving

and allow your body to recover?"

I shrug. "I guess I don't do that very well."

"I didn't think so. You need to start—the sooner the better. You have to let your body recover from everything you're putting it through. Otherwise, you're not going to have enough energy for competition."

"I feel lazy when I just sit around, though."

"That's an interesting belief. Where did you learn that?"

I shrug. "I don't know. I've always thought it."

"Probably not. You learned it somewhere."

I remembered one summer, when I was still in junior high school, I was resting on the couch on a Saturday morning. The sun was shining brightly through the windows into our front room overlooking the street. I felt the rays warming my face when I heard the front door open and my father emerged. He peered around the corner at me and shared that he had already completed his run for the day—sixteen miles, I believe. I felt ashamed and lazy for relaxing. I cringe and erase the memory from my mind.

"I'm not sure," I say, being only partially truthful.

"Keep thinking about it. You'll have plenty of time, now that you'll be resting a little more and training just a little less."

"Training less? I can't train less. All my competition trains like I do. They'll beat me if I train less."

"Lisa," Dr. Connor lowers her tone and leans forward on her desk. "They're beating you now."

I stare at her. I pick up a pencil and toy with it; a minute ticks by on the clock. "How much less?"

"Not too much. We're just going to make your sessions a little more targeted and a little shorter. Increase the intensity, decrease the duration. Do you think you can do that?"

"If it's not working, I'm going back to my way."

She moves to her filing cabinet again and pulls out a new sheet of paper. "Here's what I suggest. Omit the longer-distance running. That's probably not sport-specific enough. Instead, go to the dome and try some interval training: wind sprints, 100-yard dashes, stuff like that. Time yourself or get someone else to do it. In addition, add some Plyometric work like cone hops, box jumps, and bounding. Get the guys in the athletic department to help you. They eat this kind of thing up. You'll see a difference in a few weeks, I guarantee it."

I take the piece of paper with the exercises clearly written on it. "How long should the sessions be?"

"Not long. Twenty minutes at the most to start and then work up to thirty minutes. The key is intensity with alternating rest. You're a well-conditioned athlete, so you'll advance quickly, but you have to give yourself a little time."

I nod and digest the information.

"The other thing I want you to do is to plan your training so that you peak at the tournament, not burn out before it. You should be doing minimal physical activity about three days prior to the tournament."

"I should stop going to practice?"

"No, but when you go, drill lightly, but stay focused."

I sigh audibly. "I can't believe I'm agreeing to this. It goes against everything I believe in."

"You have to make it work, Lisa."

"What about the mental training?"

"I'm glad you mentioned it. In addition to the physical training, you should focus on mental training and relaxation," she says and pulls the symptom sheet back out of my file. "I was looking over these again. We've talked about triggering to help you manage the focusing problem. I'm hoping that some of the physical symptoms, like the butterflies and the nausea, will subside when you can focus more. But you have to practice the techniques, Lisa. It's like anything else."

"I hope you're right."

Dr. Connor rises to walk me to the door. "I hope so, too."

17

November 1992
Phoenix, Arizona
Sunkist International Open Tournament

The clock shows one o'clock in the morning. I have to fall asleep. Laurel lies in the bed across from me, sound asleep and probably dreaming. She joined me in Phoenix for the tournament and her support is especially welcomed since neither my mom nor my dad are in attendance this time, though admittedly, their presence makes me more nervous.

I have followed all of Dr. Connor's instructions: the training schedule, the tapering, and the nutritionist. I am at a solid 103 pounds—no cutting weight and no starving. I have practiced the focusing techniques over and over in the training room, visualized my wrestling matches continuously, winning every time. I didn't cut an ounce of weight; it just dropped off naturally with the right food and the training. It seems I've done everything right. But something is still so wrong.

I turn sideways to get comfortable and close my eyes. I breathe deeply, reminding myself to relax. *There is nothing else to do now.* In my mind's eye, I see the wrestling mats and the fans, the blazing spotlights and me in my singlet. I cannot see my opponent clearly, but she is represented by an obscure collection of wild movements. I hear her fan section clearly cheering madly. My muscles jerk in reaction to the visualization. My shoulders are tense, my abdomen is flexed and my forehead is furrowed.

"Are you awake?" my sister whispers. Her voice startles me; I think I am the only one up.

"Wide awake," I respond and turn toward her voice.

"What time do you wrestle tomorrow?"

"First session is at nine o'clock in the morning. We'll wrestle throughout the day and finals will probably be at seven."

"I'll bet you'll be in the finals," she says and winks at me. I smile back at her. We lie in the dim light for a moment.

"Are you nervous?" She asks.

I so wish I could say no. But the nerves, the butterflies, the sleeplessness, it's all the same. Nothing is different than before.

"What else is new," I answer. I hear rustling in her bed and my eyes begin to adjust to the darkness.

She sits up and then feels her way over to my bed. "How come you're nervous? I know you're gonna do really well," she offers.

"It's not so much that I don't think I'll do well. Or maybe it is, I don't know anymore." It seems like such a simple question, and I wish it had a simple answer. I prop myself up on one arm. "Sometimes I'm just out-skilled. I can live with that. But most of the time, I lose because I beat myself. I get out on the mat and fall apart. I'm tight, I'm timid, and I'm unfocused. It's a really helpless feeling. It's so frustrating. When I get to tournaments, I look like I haven't seen the smooth side of a mat before. I'm a completely different athlete in the wrestling room. It's so embarrassing." My confession surprises me. I flop back down on the mattress.

"Don't you think you're being a little hard on yourself?" She asks.

I sigh deeply. "No, I don't. I just expect a lot of myself."

"I expect a lot of myself, too, but I balance it with realism. You're not being rational. How can you be embarrassed about getting out on a mat in front of thousands of people and wrestling? Ninety percent of the people who will watch you tomorrow couldn't last thirty seconds doing what you do."

I shake my head. "It's not about what other people can do. It's about what I can do."

"But you measure yourself against some kind of superhuman. And in that way, it *is* about what other people can do. You think you have to be a thousand times better than the average person."

Her words linger in the air. Darkness looms. Something about her comment nags at me.

"Lisa?"

"Yeah?"

"I love you no matter what happens tomorrow, okay?"

I choke back a tear welling in the vulnerable place I keep hidden, mostly from myself. "I love you, too."

The arena is cool and dry as I bend down to secure the laces on my yellow wrestling shoes. I am wrestling on the center mat before a crowd of several hundred. Laurel is in my corner on a folding chair; a genuine smile is fixed on her face. My opponent and I lurk in the center of the mat, awaiting the referee. I feel self-doubt creeping into the vastness of my mind. It threatens to suck the confidence out of me. I turn away from the crowd, away from Laurel, and into the other corner. I breathe a stream of cold air in and out of my lungs with deliberation and then force my palms together with a loud clap. *Focus. Focus. Focus.* I clap again—the trigger. I say it over and over, a mantra in my head. When I am convinced of it, the crowd's hold over me diminishes, the cold air seems warmer, and feeling returns to my fingers. I continue until the referee's whistle sounds.

"Let's go, Lisa," I hear Laurel shout. "You can do this," she says, and claps her hands several times.

These are the last words I hear as I tune out the sounds. I turn to my opponent, already in wrestling stance and muscles tight, and clap my hands one last time directly in her face. I feel more confident than I ever have before. The referee's hand waves high in the air and the whistle chirps with a sharp bite to begin the match. I talk to myself confidently, tell myself to relax and stay in good position. I feel more connected to myself, to my body, than I ever have in a wrestling match before.

We battle for position in the center of the mat, pushing and pulling each other's body weight, each of us determined get the first points. She butts my head with hers, but I am unmovable. I push her shoulders and stay in defensive position. Her gestures to the coach in her corner reveal her mounting frustration. I block her offense several times and she gets timid. She takes one too many steps backward and the referee signals passivity, a penalty. The action breaks and momentarily, the sound in the arena returns.

"Good job, Lisa, stay in there," I hear Laurel say. I manage a sharp half smile, in spite of myself.

My opponent must now start on all fours, not a desired position, and the referee signals the match to start again. I drop on top of her, covering her hips and head. She is squirming to get out from underneath but I weave my leg underneath hers and crank her off the ground. Her shoulder is open and waiting for me to grab it. I hear her beneath me, grunting, struggling, but I expose her back to the mat and I score the first points of the match.

"Two points," the referee indicates to the judges in my favor. I try the same move again, but this time, she has learned better. The referee brings us back to our starting position after ten seconds of no action. The whistle blows and the pummeling begins again.

As quickly as I have gained my points, I lose the advantage. The move she executes is not in my repertoire and I have no defense for it. She takes me to my back faster than I can get my legs beneath me and I am struggling not to get pinned. It is a close call but I fight to my belly, safely out of harm but still in poor position. She wraps a bony arm beneath my shoulder and cranks on it, twisting my body in half. My ribs rub together I am sure, and pain shoots through my sides. I cannot breathe but I fight out from under to my belly again. I pop my head up with exaggeration attempting to keep her from trying the same thing twice. She receives three points for her move. I am behind in the match.

And so it remains until the final whistle. When the referee signals that we are out of time, I climb to my feet as my opponent raises both hands in victory. I saunter over to her coach and shake his hand. I am going through the motions, though. Another match lost—another bewildering experience.

Laurel is waiting in my corner for me when I arrive. She wears a grin of pride and hugs me.

"You looked so good, Lisa. You really did." She hands me my warm ups.

"Thanks," I say, between heaves of breath.

"That clapping thing was cool," she says and mimics me. "You intimidated me and I wasn't even wrestling you."

"It didn't work as well as I would have liked," I say as I slip my pants on.

"Why do you say that?"

"I lost."

"I still think you did great. I'm proud of you. You look so much better than last year. Really, it's amazing."

I nod my head but the self-praise won't come. "It's just not there," I say to myself. I search inside for some measure of satisfaction or pride. Laurel picks up my gym bag for me and I lead us away, the whistles growing faint.

Several hours later, I stand atop the podium. I bend down to receive my third place medal as the crowd looks on, none of them knowing the churning of my stomach nor the breaking of my heart.

18

November 1992
Cedar Falls, Iowa

"It was probably the most relaxed I've ever been," I say to Dr. Connor. "I'm not saying it was easy, but the trigger worked pretty well."

"I'm so glad to hear that," she says. "You should be proud of yourself." She beams from ear to ear on her long, sculpted face.

"I should be, shouldn't I?" I look down at the floor and swing my legs back and forth.

"But you're not?" She asks.

I look out the window as the snow falls lightly on the tops of the brick buildings. The peacefulness of it seems so foreign, so far away.

"I'm not proud of myself. I'm mad at myself."

"Why?"

"Because I still didn't do it, really. On the outside, I probably looked like I was mentally collected. And on the inside, I was much more calm and focused than I usually am. But I still couldn't get myself to believe—" I stop myself. The words are painful to say and my heart won't allow it.

"Believe what?"

I chew on the inside of my lip. I look around the room, hoping for some reprieve. There is none.

"I don't believe—I just—I'm not convinced."

"Not convinced of what?"

I struggle. I am ashamed, embarrassed. I look down again. I recall the tournament, my stepping out on the mat. "I did all the new training you suggested: the mental stuff, the triggers, the Plyometrics, the tapering. All the stuff I was supposed to do. I really felt prepared to make this tournament different. Then, when it came time for the match, I was out there, just standing on the mat waiting for the match to start, and this phrase pops in my head. I don't know where it came from."

"What was the phrase?"

I sigh and look out the window again. At first I stall, but in the end, it seems pointless. "It was, 'I'm not good enough.'"

Dr. Connor nods. "That is unfortunate," she agrees. "What do you think it means?"

I throw my hands in the air. "Hell if I know. Probably that I don't think I'm good enough to beat anybody, I guess. I have no idea. I do know that I'm getting fed up feeling like this."

"I would imagine so."

"I feel like I'm wasting your time, too. You're working so hard to help me. But the bottom line is that I have got to start believing that I am good enough to win—otherwise I'm wasting everyone's time."

Dr. Connor studies me carefully but says nothing. Finally, she asks, "Would you like to give me a call when you want to talk again?"

"That would probably be best. I just have some things to figure out first."

She nods. "I understand." She rises to walk me out and we both pause in the doorway.

"Thanks for everything you've done to help me," I say. "Please understand that this has nothing to do with you."

"I know. I'm not going to say I'm not disappointed, but I understand you have a lot going on right now."

I nod and start for the handle, but Dr. Connor stops me.

"I'd like to show you something before you go." She slips over to the filing cabinet and pulls out the familiar green sheet with the anxiety symptoms. It is not mine, though; it is the one she had shown me earlier in the year, the one of another athlete. "Do you remember when I showed this to you? You had said her symptoms looked like yours?"

"How could I forget?"

"Do you remember what you asked me about her?"

I recall the conversation. "I think I asked something about

her anxiety keeping her from playing her sport. Is that what you mean?"

She nods. "I told you that she was never able to control it, remember? That she had stopped playing because of it?"

"Sure, I remember."

She sets the paper down on the bookshelf. "The athlete was me."

A lump develops in my throat. "The athlete is you?"

"Was me – past tense. I never competed after that year because I couldn't control those symptoms you see scratched all over the page. Absolutely paralyzed me."

I return to my chair. My head spins with questions. "But why? Why couldn't you control it? Couldn't anyone help you?"

"I suppose a lot of people could have, but I wouldn't let them."

"Why not?"

"A lot of reasons. None of them good ones. Mostly because I was never able to really admit to myself or anyone else what the anxiety was all about."

"What do you mean?"

"Lisa, no one but you can tell you what is really going on in your head, in your body, as an athlete. Everyone is different. But the anxiety is your body, your mind, trying to tell you something and someday, you're going to have to really listen."

I swallow hard to speak. "I'm really sorry you quit basketball. If you loved it half as much as I love wrestling, then you're a brave person for letting go."

She opens the door for me again. "First of all, I never let go; I just stopped hanging around basketball because it was too painful. Secondly, the brave thing to do would have been to face whatever it was."

I pass through the doorway and she hands me her business card.

"Instead," she concludes, "I ran away."

116

19

January 1993
Cedar Falls, Iowa

Snowfall becomes a slushy wet mess as I peer outside the tall picture windows of the gym where I work on Main Street. I abandon my view to answer a shrilling phone at the front desk.

"Girl," the voice says triumphantly. It is Roye Oliver, the United States' women's wrestling developmental coach. His voice is as bright as I remember it, and it is an appealing contrast in this rugged man. I have always been fond of Coach Oliver; he was my first national level coach and his devotion to women's wrestling distinguishes him from his colleagues.

"Sorry to mess witcha at work, but you even harder to reach at home than I am."

"I know, I'm sorry. I'm always training or at class."

"Thas okay. So you wanna go wrestle in Sweden or what?"

"Are you serious?"

"You darn right I'm serious, girlie."

"I don't get it. I placed third at the Sunkist International in November."

"True, but you the second place American and that qualify you for the overseas developmental tournament to wrestle for the USA. So you goin' with us?"

My heart pounds. I can hardly get the words out. "Of course I'm going. What do I need to do?"

"Jes tell me you can be at the camp on Febwary 5th in Phoenix. We train for a week and then we fly to Sweden."

"How much will this cost me?"

"Girl, it don't cost you nothin'. USA wrestlin' pay for everything. This is serious business, girl. France, Sweden, Norway—everybody gonna be there. Can we count on you?"

"I'll see you in Phoenix, Coach."

"'Thas my girl. Aright then, look for a ticket in the mail next week. Talk to ya then."

"Coach?"

"Yeah, girlie?"

"Thanks."

"Aright then. Now you get in that room of yours and train." I hang up the phone. The sounds of triumph trumpet through my head and I revel in the fact that this dream of mine might just come true after all.

My hand is shaking when I dial Steve's number.

"I was just about to call you," he says. "I have some news."

"I do too!"

"You sound excited," he says. "You go first."

"I'm going to wrestle in Sweden," I shout, giggling like a child. "I can't believe it!"

"I'm really happy for you. That's really great, honey. Really." Something in his voice lingers.

"What's your news?" I ask the question cautiously.

"Not as good as yours, I'm afraid."

"What's the matter?"

He pauses. "I got my student teaching assignment."

"And?"

"And it's in Council Bluffs, where my mom lives, four hours from here. "

"Four hours? That's a long commute."

He pauses again. "I don't think I'm going to commute, actually." He breathes a loud sigh. "I think the easiest thing would be to move in with my mom for the semester."

I say nothing and he tries to fill the silence. "Just for a semester, until the student teaching is complete."

My heart sinks into my stomach. All the self-protection and the guarding, all the rejection of him seemed worth it somehow, if only to spare me the pain of his leaving now.

"When do you go?" I whisper.

"I leave tomorrow."

"Why so soon?"

"A student teacher who was originally planning to go to Council Bluffs dropped out of the program, so they need to fill it. I was next in line."

"Can I come say goodbye to you tonight?" I squeak the words out.

"I'll be here." He says.

20

February 1993
Cedar Falls, Iowa

Icy sleet and frozen rain cover the short driveway leading up to Steve's front door. Crisp air seeps into my lungs and weighs heavy as I wait for him to answer my knock. A dim living room light switches on and Steve appears. He welcomes me inside with a hug and kiss. I cannot help but resist slightly, protecting myself from the pain of knowing it will be the last embrace from him for a while.

He pulls out a chair for me and lights a candle on the kitchen table.

"I know you like these," he says, as the small candle flickers and reflects on the white walls.

I smile and nod. "Thanks," I say and hold my hands around the candleholder. "It's cold out there."

"Do you want another sweatshirt to wear?" He asks, and rises to get me one.

"No, that's okay. "

But he is already dashing up the stairs. He returns with a sweatshirt and wraps it around my shoulders. "And you don't have to give it back when you leave. Keep it, okay? I'll get it when I come back from Council Bluffs."

I push my arms through the sleeve holes. "Perfect fit," I say.

"Do you mean the sweatshirt or us?" He teases, but I avoid the question.

"Are you all ready to go?"

"No, I haven't packed anything yet. I always wait until the last minute to do that stuff. I have a ton of laundry to do—anyway, I don't want to talk about it." He places a warm hand on mine. "I'm really going to miss you. I wish I didn't have to go right now."

"Yeah," I say. I am uncomfortable with the closeness. "But I know you're going to be a great teacher. You're going to do a great job."

"And you're going to kick some Swedish butt, right?"

"Promise." I sigh deeply. "Steve, I hate good-byes so I'm just going to make this really short." I rise out of the chair.

"You're not going already, are you?"

"Staying only postpones the inevitable, and I'm not into prolonging it."

Steve slowly shakes his head and sits silent for a moment. When he finally speaks, he is distant and pensive. "You have a lot of trouble accepting what I'm trying to give you."

"And what is that?" I furrow my brow.

"Caring, sensitivity, sincerity. Take your pick. None of it seems to be on your list of things to pay attention to."

"That's not true." I sit back and cross my arms.

"Isn't it? Unless it has something to do with wrestling, you don't seem to be interested."

"That's not true either. I showed up to say good-bye, didn't I?"

"Yeah, you showed up. But you're not really here."

I roll my eyes. "What does that mean?"

"You know what I'm talking about. You're going through the motions, but you're not experiencing any of it." He tilts his head. "What are you afraid of?"

"This is ridiculous. I'm not afraid of anything."

"Oh, come on, Lisa." He scoffs. "Everyone's afraid of something."

"Well, I'm sorry to disappoint you, but I'm not." I push my chair out from the table. "I'll be in Phoenix for a week and then in Sweden, so I guess we won't be talking to each other for a while."

"Not necessarily. I can be reached at my Mom's house for the next four months." He shifts in his chair. "Do you want the phone number?"

I study him. The light from the candle flickers in his eyes and wisdom that I do not have shines through them. I wait too long to answer.

"Fine. I'm not playing this game with you." He scribbles the number on a piece of scratch paper. "Here. Use it or don't use it. It's up to you." He slides the paper across the table.

I take the number. I jingle my car keys and head for the doorway. His caring and goodness trail behind me, pulling at me. He pauses in the entryway as I push open the storm door exposing myself to the open air. The pain of leaving this way pierces me and I struggle to find a way to connect with him without admitting the need to. If only I knew why accepting his love is so difficult for me.

"Thanks for the sweatshirt," I say, knowing it is a weak attempt at connection. I hug him, reserving some energy to fight the tears that are sure to come as soon as I leave him. He hugs back with all his strength, as I knew he would.

21

February 1993
Phoenix, Arizona

An appetite for warm Phoenix weather does not go unsatisfied as I stand with a crowd of impatient strangers awaiting taxis at the airport. Bursts of hot wind slap my cheeks as I peer down the access road in front of the baggage claim wondering how long I'll be pacing in my sweatpants and sweatshirt.

When I finally climb into the yellow cab, perspiration is draining down my chest and it's odd how used to it I am. The driver ignores my overdone outfit and delivers me to the hotel adjacent to the wrestling facility. I am wilted when I get to my room, but the air-conditioning inside gives me just enough refreshment to unpack and dig through my suitcase for cooler clothes.

I am half dressed when I hear rustling outside the door and a key turning in the lock. I race for cover around the corner, as the door creaks open and hits against the wall.

"Hey, roomie," she shouts. I hear the thud of a suitcase on the bed. "I saw you streakin'. Come out and introduce yourself."

I pull the t-shirt over my head and reappear, somewhat startled by this awkward introduction.

"I'm Jimi from Oklahoma." Her eyes widen and a smile emerges from one side of a spherical face to the other. She looks around the room.

"Lisa Whitsett from Iowa," We shake hands.

"What was the last name?"

"Whitsett."

"Whatsit?"

"No, Whit-sett." I over-enunciate.

She tries it again, but cannot mimic it. "That's a weird last name."

"What's yours?" I fire back.

"Hornbuckle."

I shake my head. "Hornbuckle? That's not weird?"

"Hey, it's Native American." On her bed perches an enormous green suitcase with a broken zipper and a duct taped handle. She flips open the top. "And you better watch it, Lisa from Iowa. 'Cause I'm one crazy Indian."

I believe the crazy part.

"What weight do you wrestle?" I ask, sitting down across from her.

"One hundred thirty-four. I'm carrying a lot of extra water right now though; I just had a baby a few months ago. Makes cutting weight a lot harder, that's for sure."

I'm impressed that she's on the mat so soon.

She rummages through a bag. "I've got new pictures of him," she says, as she brings me a handful of snapshots. "His name is Dakota."

I flip through the pictures. "He's got your eyes, doesn't he?"

"And a whole lot more," she agrees, gathering the pictures. "So what do you weigh?" She asks me.

"One hundred and three."

"Skinny. Are you on weight?"

"Yeah, I think so. I checked the scale downstairs. It looks pretty good. Then again, I've been fooled before."

"What time does practice start?"

I check my watch and curse. "Three minutes ago."

"Hey, girlies. You're late," Coach Oliver announces with a smile. Jimi and I drop our bags in a corner, still panting from the run.

"Thanks for noticing, Coach. Good to see you, too." For a moment I am concerned he'll be truly upset with us, but a glance around the room at the other wrestlers distracts me. Shannon Williams—the one who had knocked me out at Nationals—wrestling up one weight at 116 pounds drills with Afsoon Roshanzamir, the 103-pound wrestler who had won the Sunkist International in November. At 97 pounds, Marie

Prado drills with Tricia Saunders, now wrestling at 110 pounds.

A man I do not recognize lingers in the corner, scribbling on a clipboard. He looks up when Jimi and I dash in, but he seems less concerned than Coach Oliver and instead resumes his scribbling. Coach Oliver finally greets me with a hug, asks me if I'm on weight, and then hustles me to the corner.

"Coach, this is Lisa Whitsett, our other 103 pounder. Lisa, this is Coach Sergio Gonzalez, he and I will be coaching this team."

"Glad you made it in, Lisa." Coach Gonzalez says. He can't be taller than me, maybe even an inch shorter. I would be surprised if he weighed as much. But his neck and forearms were sinewy and strong, and it was a welcomed change to have a coach I might actually be able to work out with.

"I understand you've known Coach Oliver for some time."

"Yes, sir." I shake his hand, noticing mine is clammy.

"That's okay, you don't have to call me Sir. Coach Gonzalez is fine. "

I concede.

"Excited for the tournament?"

"Very."

"Me, too. I haven't coached a women's team before. I'm really looking forward to it."

I want to believe him.

"My coaching style may be a little different than what you're used to," he started. He didn't know I had no coach. Any style is better than no style.

"I think this team has the potential to do really well, but I know because of the level of competition at women's tournaments, you guys are probably getting away with some stuff that you shouldn't be."

"What do you mean?"

"Don't misunderstand me. My point is that I teach the basics of wrestling – particular the importance of good position. A lot of these girls here are silver medallists, gold medallists – but they still don't practice the basics enough. My goal is to get you guys to focus on that. Trust me, it's the difference between good and great."

It occurs to me that some of the wrestlers on our team might not like hearing that they were getting lucky on the mat rather than using good position and technique, but Coach Gonzales is right. It would be interesting seeing others' reactions. Meanwhile, I just feel grateful to have a coach.

"Take a few minutes to warm up. When you're ready, we're gonna work." I obey and drop to the mat to stretch. He turns to pay attention to some of the other wrestlers, already drilling on a neighboring mat. I hear him coaching, "Basics, Marie, basics…"

The first traces of nervousness trickle through my blood.

A sweeping glance through our wrestling room just one week later reveals the impact of our coaches' and our team's efforts. Even the more experienced wrestlers looked a little more polished, and the less experienced wrestlers were more developed in their styles and their aggressiveness. With few exceptions, everyone has worked hard, and it shows.

Coach Gonzalez bellows to us the day of our final practice before the trip. "Line up on the wall by weight. We'll go in two groups, light to middleweights first. Give me hard sprints down one side of the room and then back. Keep sprinting until I tell you when to stop." He checks his watch. "Let's go."

My team and I are horses on a track, galloping and pounding, heaving and sweating. We race each other from one end of the room to another, mentally setting our sights on Sweden. Sweat drips off our legs and arms, creating slick spots on the mats. After numerous laps, we continue to reach for the wall and groan at the pain of burning lungs and screaming quads. We never slow down.

At the end of twenty minutes, our coach calls time. We jog around the room, lungs certainly on fire.

"Good job, team," Coach Gonzalez yells out with encouragement and stops his watch. "Had enough for today?" Some athletes nod and slow to a walk, but Shannon and I still jog clockwise as our bodies recover quickly from the sprints.

"One more round, Coach," Shannon suggests as she rounds

the corner toward Coach Gonzalez. He wrinkles his forehead.

"Two more minutes of sprints, Coach," I agree as I pick up my jogging pace again. Only a few of the junior wrestlers groan at the suggestion and look at Coach as if he were a judge sentencing defendants. Coach Gonzalez glances at Coach Oliver who shrugs his shoulders in agreement.

"Let's go then. Two minutes; make it good," Coach Gonzalez sets his stopwatch again and leans against the wall. He whispers something to Coach Oliver and they both smile. They both know they have prepared us well, and the United States is ready.

Our coaches have an easy time corralling us the next day in preparation for the trip to Sweden. The fatigue we feel from the week's practices lingers but is overshadowed by the anticipation of the tournament. For some of our team members including me, it is our first opportunity to wrestle overseas. At 9:00 a.m. on Tuesday, February 8, Team USA, our coaches, and our trainer board an airplane bound for the other side of the world.

22

February 1993
Klippan, Sweden

Thirteen hours of flight time temper our excitement, and I struggle to fill the time with long naps, silly conversation, and Disney movies. Jimi calls her mom from the air, asking to speak with Dakota who was roused from his nap to talk to her. She tells him all about the big plane she was riding in and promises to bring him back a set of wings he asked for.

Our plane finally descends into an airport in Copenhagen, Denmark. The time zone changes have caught up with most of us, and I am certainly feeling the jetlag. A ferry ride to Klippan, Sweden caps off the trip, and the beauty of both countries cannot be ignored even at the early morning hour when we arrive. Klippan's buildings are massive stone structures with pillars and pointy rooftops including the churches that are erected on nearly every corner. The narrow streets are dotted with old-fashioned street signs, lampposts, and traffic signals. Bakeries and small retail shops line the sidewalks. Old theatres that still hold live productions draw large crowds, despite the long lines.

We congregate in the lobby of Hotel Klippan awaiting our room assignments. Jimi and I hunch over our suitcases with our eyes closed, hoping to catch some sleep. I open my eyes only once when I hear commotion from our team mascot, a retired medical doctor who now sponsors some of our wrestlers and often travels with us. His support is unmatched but his manner amusing; he is absolutely graceless. This time, a piece of paper has escaped from his briefcase and the doctor is pursuing it in a circle, like a dog chasing its tail. I giggle silently to myself with my eyes closed until I hear Jimi laughing, too. Then we both burst into a roar.

Half an hour later and shamefully past our bedtime, the lobby is still flooded with our suitcases and duffel bags.

Coach Gonzalez calls for our attention. "Our rooms aren't ready yet, so grab your workout stuff; let's head over to the training room."

No one moves because we think he is kidding. With the time zone change, it is four o'clock in the morning for team USA. The last thing we are ready to do is wrestle. But Coach Gonzalez is not kidding, it turns out, and before I have a chance to think about how much I want my head on a hotel pillow, I am jogging over to the wrestling room a few blocks away.

Some of our competitors are wrestling when we arrive. Others have completed their workouts and now walk the hall-ways pointing at pictures of female wrestlers that line the corridor. The training center is modest but comfortable, and I am intrigued that a public facility so openly encourages female participation in the sport.

Coach Gonzalez leads us through our traditional warm-up and before long, Team USA is drilling hard again. I am paired with Marie Prado. Neither of us speaks about the time of night or our fatigue and instead, we remain concentrated and focused, working our technique with automatic execution. Both of us have our rhythm when Marie hits a single leg takedown to my left side. I throw my hips in to counter her move, but my right shoe sticks to the mat. One hundred and three pounds of force twist my leg and pain shoots through my body.

"Damn it!" I go down screaming, grabbing the inside of my leg, which feels like it has snapped in two.

Marie drops to my side and spouts apologies and questions. "Are you okay? Lisa, I'm sorry. What happened?"

I writhe on the mat and wave her off.

Our trainer, Dave, rushes over to us. "What is it, where does it hurt?"

I exhale deeply and manage to squeak out a few words. "My leg. The inside."

"Like your groin muscle?" He places both hands near my upper thigh.

"Right here," I scowl and lay back, trying to breathe through it.

"Alright. It's okay. Just relax."

"Relax? My leg is on fire and the tournament is in two days."

"I know, I know, just breathe." Dave hunches over me. "It's gonna be okay.

Now show me what position makes it hurt the most."

"Show you? Why the hell would I do that?"

"Because then we'll tape it to make sure it doesn't go that way," Dave insists.

I lay my head back down. "I'm trusting you on this."

"I know," he says. "Show me."

Marie and Dave support me as I hobble to the next room. I bite my lip and demonstrate the position until I feel the muscle resist again. Dave requests that Marie stay in the room as a protective measure; he was, after all, about to tape up my groin.

"That way, we'll both feel more comfortable doing this," he smiles.

When the wrapping is over, I return to the mat, still hobbling but determined to keep moving. I drill very lightly at Dave's suggestion, trying to keep the muscle warm but not overusing it. I do not sprint with the rest of our team at the close of practice. Instead I bike at the same interval time as they sprint. Dave assures me I will get the same benefit. I have no choice but to believe him.

Frosty air stirs and snow falls lightly on the narrow sidewalks as we crawl back to the hotel, sweaty and yearning for warm showers. Jimi and I retrieve our luggage from the storage area and climb wearily to our room, now ready to be occupied. My groin muscle aches with nearly every step.

We push open the creaking door to reveal the most minuscule, narrow room we have ever seen. The television, dresser, and two modest cots barely fit in the confines of the space. Some seasoned international wrestlers inform me later that having a bathroom in each room is a luxury. That night, I convince Jimi to take a picture of me with my arms outstretched, proving that I can reach from one side to another.

The morning arrives along with clouds and a murky sky. Jimi still sleeps. I lay in my cot, wondering who else is awake and thinking about the tournament. I have forgotten for a moment about my leg but am reminded instantly when I take my first giant step toward the closet to pull on warm sweats and a hooded sweatshirt.

Descending the stairs with care, I pass a room that looks as if it has been prepared for wrestlers. Two electronic scales, which I will visit shortly, are erected in a corner, and a private changing area flanks them. I wave good morning to the front desk receptionist and wander into the breakfast area. Dark coffee is already brewed and waiting for me on the breakfast bar. Shortly after I have filled my second cup, Jimi wanders into the room.

"How much?" She asks, sipping.

"For the coffee? It's free," I say, with my eyes still half shut.

"No, not the coffee. How much do you weigh?"

"I'm on weight, I think. I didn't check yet. What about you?"

"Don't know. I need to get on a scale," she says hesitantly and rubs her eyes. I escort her to the room I have discovered. Jimi hops onto the scale fully clothed. She stares at the digital numbers bouncing back and forth until they finally settle.

"Uh-oh," she whispers.

"What's the matter?" I ask.

Jimi steps off the scale, then on again. She does not respond and jumps off and on the scale several times.

"Jimi, what's the matter?" I repeat.

She rips her clothes off piece by piece until she stands in nothing but her underwear. She stares at the numbers and then looks at me, pale faced.

I limp around behind her to view the scale. Jimi wrestles at 134 pounds. The scale shows 141.

"Damn," I say when I see the bright red numbers. "Get your plastics on. Let's go."

"I was thinking the same thing," Jimi groans. I grab my

lucky stocking cap from upstairs and together we bulldoze into the sting of the Swedish winter.

It has been more than a year since I have sworn off weight cutting. The whole experience at Nationals cured me of it, but I really want to help Jimi. Her real challenge is not to lose too much too soon. If she does, she will probably drink it all back and have to cut the weight all over again. Keeping this in mind, Jimi runs for about thirty minutes while I hobble behind her until our noses are so cold we can no longer breathe. We retreat to the hotel with a new tactic.

"Jimi, keep your plastics on and keep jumping," I instruct. "Your homemade sauna will be ready soon." Jimi nods and I limp upstairs to our room. I turn the shower knob marked H as far as it will go and shut the door tightly. I hop back down the stairs to find Jimi jogging in place.

"Let's go, Jimi. Upstairs," I direct.

Jimi has done this a thousand times before, but I imagine that after having a baby, it might be harder. The weight doesn't come off any faster with two people focused on it, but it hurts a little less. I check the bathroom temperature, so hot I can hardly breathe.

"I hate you," Jimi announces before opening the door to the bathroom.

"Don't hate me yet, " I suggest. "If you haven't lost four pounds by the end of this, then you can hate me, because that means we're hitting the bikes next."

Jimi groans and shuts the door behind us. We sit together, she on the end of the tub and me in a corner on the floor.

Our trainers hate to see us do this to ourselves. We all pretend that we can drink it all back the next day, but that is physiologically impossible. None of us wrestles better after cutting weight. I learned that the hard way. We are more fatigued and have no food in our systems. So after weight cutting, it is just a gut match. It comes down to who can wrestle the best, the longest, the smartest, without giving in mentally. Four minutes seems like a short time if you're riding in a car. When you're wrestling, it seems like a decade.

My groin feels a little better from the heat but I need a break.

I decide to step into the hall to see who else is awake now. One of our wrestlers, Dana Wells, yells to me from her room.

"Hey, do you have a hat?"

"Are you over?" I am curious who else would be visiting the sauna.

"By two pounds, and I don't float anything." I sympathize with her. Certain people just wake up a pound or two lighter than they are when they go to sleep. Wrestlers call it floating weight. But not every wrestler is so lucky.

I think about my lucky stocking cap. It is the only hat I have and the only one I ever wear. I never loan it to anyone. The last time I loaned out my wrestling gear, it never found its way back to me. On the other hand, Dana is my teammate, and I want to help her if I can.

"I'll lend you my cap. But you have to understand that if I don't get this back, I'll kill you. It's my lucky hat and I have to wear it before I wrestle."

Dana doesn't laugh; she recognizes superstition.

"I only have to be in the sauna for about half an hour. I'll bring it back right after."

"I'll be over there, too, so just find me."

I give the stocking cap away with a secret plan to go after it if Dana isn't back in the thirty she promised. I return to check on Jimi. She has been sweating for a while and it is probably about time to check her weight again.

We run across the road to the training room, which is open now and home to a line of female wrestlers waiting to check their weight. Jimi is still jumping up and down trying to shed water. Rather than wasting precious time in line, I jog around the wrestling room a little trying to warm up my leg and hope that Jimi will follow me. Eventually, she does.

"You look good," I say after several laps, trying to sound positive.

Jimi can see through the façade and rolls her eyes. "How long have we been jogging?"

"Let's see," I say, glancing at my watch. "Do you want to count our jog over here or just the actual laps around the gym?"

"I mean how long, counting any activity I've done after we

left the hotel, in which I moved my legs or arms in any way and possibly lost weight, have I been jogging?"

"I would say, counting the jog over, about seven minutes."

Jimi drops her head.

"I know that sucks. You'll float one or two tonight and whatever you're still over, you can cut in the morning."

"If I can still move in the morning."

Unfortunately, she is probably right. I choose not to point this out to Jimi, who is developing black circles under her eyes.

We have been jogging for twenty-five minutes when I spot Dana. She emerges from the sauna, hair matted to her head with sweat and dripping. She is hatless. I immediately confront her.

"Are you done?" I ask, trying not to sound too abrupt.

"Yeah, I think I lost all the weight now. "

"I mean, are you done with my hat?" The question sounds childish and desperate.

She pats the top of her head. "I must have left it in the sauna."

The sauna is packed to the walls with weight-cutting wrestlers. I elbow my way to the corner where a bench houses various pieces of clothing, sweaty plastics, and spare socks. I tear up the corner looking for it, but it does not surface. My heart rate increases and I am sweating from the heat. I turn to face the wave of wrestlers, jumping up and down. It is dimly lit and I know that someone could take my hat, hide it under her clothes, and it would never be found. I prepare to body search every wrestler when I spy the silhouette of a lone wrestler picking up an item from the corner. I shove my way through the crowd. As I get closer, I can see it is my cap. I grab the wrestler's hand as she starts to pick up the item. Clenching her wrist in my sweaty hand, I realize that she is only moving it aside to sit in its place. My apology for attacking her is sincere but I cannot help feeling more secure with my hat safely on my head.

I burst from the sauna and turn my attention to Jimi. Her jog has slowed to a fast walk, and her feet are hardly lifting off the mat.

"Well, it's official," I say. "I've gone crazy. I just attacked another wrestler for grabbing my hat." Jimi does not respond, so I switch subjects. "Do you want to check your weight?"

"How long have I been jogging?" She asks.

"About forty minutes. Good job."

My praise does not affect her as she staggers to the scale with her hands on her hips. She removes her shoes and strips her sweatshirt and sweatpants. Jimi peels the clothes from her sweaty body until only her damp singlet remains.

"If I'm not on weight right now, tell Dakota I love him and then shoot me, cause I'm not jogging anymore." With her eyes closed, she takes in a deep breath, exhales, and places both feet upon the scale.

"Yes!" Jimi shouts.

"You made it?" I peer over Jimi's shoulder. The scale reads 137. She hasn't lost all of it, but she is only three pounds off.

"I can float one or two overnight and run off the rest tomorrow. I won't drink or eat anything tonight. "

"Way to go, girl," I slap her on the back.

"Don't you have any weight to lose?" Jimi asks with a wrinkled face.

"Nah, I'm under weight now, thanks to you."

"No way. Prove it." I realize she is only doing this to pass the time. But I humor both of us by removing my sweats and jumping on the scale.

"One hundred and two. With my shoes and sweatshirt on." I hobble off the scale and Jimi curses under her breath.

At our noon practice the following day, my leg is still not moving well. Still, I drill wrestling moves gently as Dave approaches me.

"Tired?"

I stop drilling and study him, evaluating if it is a trick question. "No." I continue drilling.

"Your back hurt?"

I do not answer. Dave has also been treating me during the trip for chronic back pain, the result of an injury I had sustained a couple years prior in the wrestling room. I was drilling with a 150-pounder, a mistake I never made again. He had locked around my leg to throw a crotch lift and was bending me in half. I did not want to stop or admit to the pain so I said nothing as muscles in my lower back ripped apart and the ligaments tore. The next day I could not straighten my back and after that, it was never the same. Ever since, I wrestle with back pain along with severely restricted torso and leg mobility.

"Leg botherin' ya?"

I stop drilling again and put my hands on my hips. "If I say it hurts are you gonna pull me from the tournament tomorrow?" I trust him to be honest.

"No," he says and crosses his arms.

I stand for a moment and then cock my head. "No, it doesn't hurt. "

Dave glances over at Coach Gonzalez who is watching the conversation from across the room. Dave shakes his head to the coach, indicating there is no problem, and turns back to me.

"Go into the weight room for a few minutes," he says in a hushed tone, "stretch it out a little bit. It's not going to hurt you now to take a break."

I raise my eyes from the mat and consider his suggestion. My leg throbs. I take one step toward the weight room before turning back around. I point at him directly.

"You better not pull me."

Dave shakes his head and I limp away.

The carpeted weight room is mirrored on all sides, making it appear larger than its true size. I sit on a flat bench and stretch my leg gently in front of me. It quivers from the strain. I am hungry, frustrated, and nervous. I place my hand on the pain, hoping to heal it somehow.

Coach Oliver appears in the doorway of the weight room. "Hey, girlie. Whas wrong?"

Seeing him startles me and I wipe a tear from my face. "Nothing's wrong."

He has always been rugged looking, but after knowing him for several years, I see the warmth beyond it. He hunches over at his waist, the result of a lower back injury he explained, and he lumbers over to me.

"Your leg hurt?" His Louisiana twang resonates deep in his throat.

I say nothing, still unsure what admitting the truth will mean for tomorrow.

"Iss gonna be okay. Jes take it easy today, get a good nigh sleep, and you be concentrating so much on wrestlin', you won' even fil it."

I nod and chew on the inside of my lip.

"You know I'm always lookin' out fe' ya," he says. I feel his hand, gentle and kind on my shoulder, a striking but welcomed contrast to the day's fierceness.

"Get up you guys." A voice yells from outside our door six-thirty the next morning.

"What the hell is that?" Jimi yanks the sheets up over her head.

"It's Coach," I reply. "Time to go weigh in."

"Yeah, right." Jimi crawls down farther in her bed.

The urgency of the moment strikes me. It is tournament day.

"Come on, get up," I say to Jimi. I go to the door and peek out. I catch Coach Gonzalez half way down the hall pounding on the others' doors.

"You know, if you keep making a racket like that, you're gonna wake someone up," I smile. He returns to our door.

"How's the leg?"

"Fine," I lie. "Feels good."

"Alright, now don't give me that. How is it really?"

"It's fine, " I lie again.

He scoffs. "Where's Jimi?"

"Dead in her bed, I think. I tried to get her up."

"Well try again and meet downstairs in thirty minutes. Time to wrestle."

I hobble back to my mattress and sit down, leg outstretched. Jimi senses I am staring at her.

"Don't get any wild ideas," I hear her announce from under the covers. "I'm getting up."

I laugh. "Coach says to meet downstairs for weigh-ins in

thirty minutes. I know I'm underweight and I want some coffee. Wanna come?"

"Coffee? You drink that stuff? I can't stand it. Besides, it's not good for you."

"It's decaf, but you're probably right," I agree. "What do you usually drink in the morning?"

"Coke."

Breakfast of champions.

Team USA members huddle together in our blue warm-ups and game faces, the tournament quickly becoming a reality. I am more agitated than I have been in weeks; the strain of the workouts, weight cutting, and traveling is showing on the faces of our team members, including Jimi's. She still does not know how much weight she has lost overnight, but the next few hours will reveal the truth.

Despite chilling winds, we parade down the main street en masse and descend on the gymnasium where we will spend the day wrestling. I stride next to Jimi who talks incessantly the whole way. For a self-described night owl, she has a lot of energy that morning. I listen unresponsively as she fantasizes about everything she wants to eat when she has weighed in, but my head is already far away and focused on the events to come.

We arrive for weigh-ins early but the corridor is already packed with other wrestling teams. I have never seen so many female wrestlers in one place and the sight of it chokes me. A few wrestlers, like Jimi, are still trying to cut some weight in the last hour by running and jumping rope. Others lay about the hallway, heads on their gym bags, focusing or catching up on sleep. Coaches and officials scurry, inspecting the grounds. The commotion plays into my uneasiness and before long, the symptoms that I have experienced at all my tournaments settle in.

And so the morning wears on, me with my nerves and Jimi with her weight cutting. Finally, at 7:30, Coach Gonzalez herds us into the weigh-in room and leaves us with the scales. I make weight easily, not realizing that I had floated a whole pound overnight. I dress quickly and collect my belongings. I indicate to Jimi that I will wait for her in the hall. She needs every last second she can get and I do not want to pressure her. At 8:30, the last possible moment a wrestler can weigh in, Jimi bursts through the double doors from the room. She emits an audible, lengthy sigh.

"It wasn't pretty, but it's done," she announces and high fives me.

Coach Gonzalez flanks her and wastes no time pulling us all together. I am grateful for the speedy round up. It's kind of like going to the dentist: once I'm in the office, I'd just as soon get in the chair rather than prolong waiting.

Coach Gonzalez's voice thunders through the hallway.

"This is it. We're weighed in and ready to go," he says, and zips up his USA warm-up jacket. My nerves twitch and my stomach rumbles.

"In the last few minutes we have together I want to say how proud I am of each one of you and how impressed I am with this team. This is the most fun I've had on a wrestling trip in a long time. I've been very impressed with your maturity, your focus and your dedication. "

"Amen, " Coach Oliver says, and nods his head.

"At 9 o'clock sharp, I want you in your USA gear lined up by that entryway across the hall. A lot of these people came here to see some awesome USA wrestling, and we're going to give them what they want."

"Thas right, girlie, relax and wrestle your way," Coach Oliver agrees, and he points at me. He is oblivious to my symptoms and pre-competition history, but I nod my head anyway, honestly promising to do so.

"Alright, now, circle up," Coach Gonzalez announces, and we huddle around him. He lowers his voice to a whisper.

"If you've never had the opportunity to yell *USA* in front of your competition, I highly recommend it." He extends his hand to the middle of our circle. "USA on three, ready?"

We each place a hand upon his.

"One, two, three," he whispers.

"U-S-A," we yell in a Marine Corps tone, much to the surprise and disgust of our opponents, particularly our rivals from France. A startled competitor turns to me, and I easily meet her eyes.

We disband to line up by the entryway where Coach Gonzalez had instructed us in preparation for the team parade around the gymnasium. One of our junior wrestlers leads the line and holds our Team USA sign high before us. Spotlights beam brilliant light and triumphant music booms over the loud speaker. *This is it*, I think to myself. *Relax. Focus.* I clap loudly as step onto the hardwood floor, my gut churning but my game face fiercely displayed.

In my first match, I locked up a tight cradle and won in less than 40 seconds. It was a great way to begin the tournament.

Belgium brought only one competitor, and she was my second match of the day. Her broad shoulders and thick legs indicated her strength, but in the end, her technique got the better of me. However, it was a low-scoring match, and that fact was encouraging to me.

The third match drew a crowd. Team France had traditionally been Team USA's rival, and this year was no different. I stepped out on the mat to meet the reigning World Champion, though I admit that I did not know that at the time. Given my tendency toward anxiety, that probably helped me. Her team swarmed the spectator area, shouting French words of encouragement. She turned to me with a game face of her own, and the adrenaline pumped through me.

I turn away from her. *Focus. Focus. Focus.* I clap my hands loudly and turn back to the center. The vastness of the arena disappears; I am not afraid today. I am in her face, pounding on her head, moving her around the mat. It was almost as if I didn't know any better. The match ends 4-2 in her favor, but I made her wrestle for it. I leave the mat and spit blood from my mouth into a bucket, noticing that France's entire team has lined the wall cheering against me.

Coach Oliver meets me at mat side. "Now, thas wrestlin', girlie." He tussles my sweaty hair, falling out of its ponytail. "Good for you."

I look down at the ground in humility, but I can't help but smile.

My last match is against another competitor from France. My teammate had beaten her earlier in the day, and this was our opportunity to put her out of the tournament.

I am warming up mat side, staying focused and concentrated. Coach Gonzales pulls me aside.

"This girl you're gonna wrestle has a bad habit of backing out of the center circle." He gets in his stance. "Remember, every time she does that, the ref is going to tell her that she has to take a step back in."

I listen closely and nod in commitment.

"When she takes that step back in, shoot on her."

When the match begins, that's exactly what I did. Coach Gonzales was right, and I scored three takedowns in the first several minutes because of it, winning the match.

I ended my first overseas tournament in fifth place at the 47-kilogram weight class. Jimi placed fifth in her weight class, too.

In the championship finals, Tricia Saunders fights to win the final match that will determine the fate of our team. Tricia locks her opponent's head and pounds her to the mat. She locks her arms tighter as her opponent struggles to regain control. Tricia exposes her opponent's back for two points and Team USA cheers wildly.

The Norwegian wrestler backs onto all fours and bursts to her feet to escape, but not before Tricia throws a crossface to the bridge of her nose, crushing it. Blood gushes onto the white mat, forcing the referee to stop the match momentarily. The Norwegian wrestler is sent to her corner to wipe off the blood pouring from her nose. The trainer shoves a piece of cotton into her nostril and the referee signals the match to commence.

The wrestlers are back on their feet, circling and lunging at one another, trying to force mistakes. The score is two to one but still in Tricia's favor. Perspiration soaks the wrestlers' singlets and hair. Their skulls collide and upon the impact, droplets of sweat rocket as far away as the next mat. Tricia's chest heaves with each breath. Bodies shoot and turn. Finally, Tricia locks the upper body of her opponent. With her final breath she collects every ounce of energy she has and takes a giant step to her right. She drops in with her hips and grips her hands together with wickedness, throwing her opponent and pounding both her shoulders to the mat for a pin. The referee's whistle shrills and the match is over. With all our combined victories, Team USA captures the Klippan Cup for the first time ever.

23

February 1993
Klippan, Sweden

Bolting upright, I bend at the waist, disoriented. When I realize I am still in Sweden, I flop backward onto my pillow. Glassy-eyed, I fixate on the sheets bound like chains around my ankles. I rip the sheets from my limbs in one practiced motion and they fall in a heap on the floor. I swivel my torso, rusty and creaking like the tin man, and dangle my sinewy legs off the edge of the bed. My groin injury throbs at this awakening, upstaged only by the acute pain in my lower vertebrae. Cracking my knuckles and twisting a tense neck, I shift to relieve the burden and survey the room.

I was too exhausted last night and in too much pain to celebrate our win, as opposed to Jimi who is not even in her bed. Evidence of her evening's celebration lay strewn about the floor including junk food wrappers, newspaper clippings, and assorted wrestling gear worn as supplementary party attire. My once-organized dresser of clothes is now a sweaty T-shirt cemetery and a dumping ground for other items that had no place to live. Empty juice bottles and banana peels in the wastecan create a potent aroma that lingers in the close quarters of our hotel room.

I drag myself out of bed and groan at the twinge of back pain. Drawing the curtains, I discover a gray-streaked Sunday sky, the same one I have seen for almost a week. My watch shows 8:00 a.m. local Sweden time, and I presume I am the first of my teammates to feel the chill that morning.

With slumberous eyelids I clutch the drapery, replaying the previous day's wrestling matches over and over in my head. My muscles twinge and flex at my vivid thoughts, what I did well, what I could have done differently, what I can do next time. I waver like a weed as I cling to the curtain.

Eventually, I drag my ragged suitcase from the corner of the room. The morning's first steps are always the most interesting of the day; today is no exception. My knees crack and pop like an arthritic eighty-year-old woman. I collect my sweaty wrestling T-shirts and socks, warm-ups, and sweatshirts. I begin folding mindlessly and my eyes transfix in a blank stare.

A rapping at the door startles me. Through the peephole I see Jimi, red-eyed with hair like Elvis, staring back at me.

"Girl, I feel horrible," she says as I open the door. She groans and falls into her bed, tripping over her suitcase.

I shut the door behind us. "And I feel the same," I agree, though I suspect it is for different reasons. I amble back to my bed, picking up my clothes slowly along the way.

"I looked around for you last night. Coach said he saw you around 10:00 and that you were too tired to come out with us." She rotates over on her side to face me. "Too good for us after your big win yesterday?"

I ball up my socks and turn my back. "Yeah, that's it. My fifth place finish rocketed me to the top of the women's wrestling circuit and now I have no room for you clowns."

"Oh, come on. You're so hard on yourself," she says, and rolls onto her stomach.

"Not hard enough I guess." This conversation sounds so familiar.

"What are you talking about? What else could you do? All you do is train. Wrestling more isn't going to make you any more of a wrestler."

I stop packing. "Jimi, don't you care at all about training? You show up at this tournament almost ten pounds overweight, which in itself is dangerous because we needed you on weight to wrestle this tournament at all. On top of that, you're the first one to say that you probably don't train enough and you don't care at all what anyone thinks about it."

Jimi stares at me. "Let me get this straight. You're pissed off because I have a life outside of wrestling, I train less than you do and I still perform well, and I wrestle because I enjoy it rather than because I need other people to tell me I'm doing something good? Forgive me, but I'm not seeing logic here."

I roll my eyes and drop back on the bed. "That's not what I meant, Jimi."

"Well, then what did you mean? Because I have to be honest with you; everything I've seen of you this week tells me you're heading straight for burnout. Your back is nearly broken in half, you're limping, and you're talking about more training when you already train three times a day at home. I don't know what you're trying to prove, but if you ask me, you're in trouble. " She pulls the blanket up over her head and turns away from me. I try unsuccessfully to get Jimi to engage, but she is stubborn.

"I'm not trying to prove anything, Jimi." I stand over her for several minutes, waiting for her to take the bait.

"My hair hurts," is all she adds, "I need to sleep."

My leg quivers from pain and finally I retreat. I gather the rest of my socks and T-shirts, throwing them violently into my suitcase. I creep toward the bathroom and bend to turn the knobs of the shower. Water pours from the spout and I undress gingerly while the water warms. I sit down on the cool linoleum floor and take several deep breaths, preparing to remove my socks. Between my groin muscle and my back, I know this will be painful. On the first bend my muscles spasm, locking my back in an upright position and pulsing with pain. I wince and recoil, try once more, and recoil again. I sit back against the wall. With my face hardened and lips pursed, I try a new tactic. I stretch my leg out in front of me and push my sock off with my opposite foot. I repeat the motion on the other side as my groin shakes with the strain. With both socks successfully off, I lay on my back and pull my knees to my chest. Droplets of sweat bead on my temples. I push one side of my pajama bottoms down one leg and then the other, kicking them off when they reach my ankles. I slide my T-shirt off over my head, free at last.

I grip the water basin to pull myself back up. Shower steam fogs over the mirror and I wipe my hand through it, catching a glimpse of my hollow-cheeked image. Once again, the steam overcomes the glass and my image slowly disappears.

Stepping carefully, I face the showerhead with my arms shoulder width apart. I lean into the hot water and my neck pops when I drop my head. My lower back throbs some more and my calves ache with bluish yellow bruises. Yes, my body is beaten up, but it has all been worth it, hasn't it? Yesterday's win was just the beginning for me. A national championship is on its way. It's exactly what I wanted all along.

These thoughts mix with the rushing water and immerse my battered body. Jimi's words nag at me like a young girl tugging on her father's leg. My jaw tightens at her suggestion that I am heading for trouble and I gnaw on the inside of my lip. *You're so hard on yourself.* The words roll around in my head like rusty pedals churning on an old bicycle. I see visions of practice after endless practice, tournament after tournament, pounding headaches and stone-faced competitors. The constant invulnerability, the toughness; all of it floods my head and gushes over my heart. The pouring shower engulfs my ears and mutes the outside sounds. Panic rises in my chest like a tidal wave. I am a volcano, erupting with the repressed disappointment, frustration, and anger that I never allow myself to feel. I clamp my hands over my mouth, choking on tears as a primal sob pours from my core. I recall the anxiety before all the tournaments, faintly covered with mental techniques that mask it but don't erase it. I overflow like lava, crying uncontrollably and gagging on the tears.

Pounding water crashes over me as the tub fills. I soak in a mixture of fatigue and sadness at what I have become. I do not even recognize myself. I hate what I see. An inflexible, blindly determined, and defensive athlete has replaced the girl I used to be: confident and secure. Emotionally, I push people away, even those who love me, too scared to ask for help, too proud to ask for support. Instead, I continue to train, continue to perform feats of athleticism, continue to exert myself in the name of my sport. Deep down, I know; I am so hard on myself. And for all my toughness, I have not had the courage to look beneath it all and ask myself why.

I lean down, staring blankly, and shut the water off. My discovery mixes with the shower mist and swallows the room.

Droplets funnel into the tub drain and I waver naked in the cold. Slowly, I wrap in a terrycloth towel and wipe the mist from the mirror with water-shriveled fingertips. The gaunt image reflects back at me. Dark circles paint the skin beneath my eyes. So many times I have peered into the mirror. Now, in this blessed moment of clarity, I am amazed at how much I am suddenly able to see.

24

February 1993
Cedar Falls, Iowa

Two weeks later, I tap on Dr. Connor's door. From inside, I hear her announce that office hours for students are tomorrow from three-thirty to five o'clock and could I please come back.

"I can't come back tomorrow," I shout through the door. "I'll be wrestling."

Papers rustle and the sound of a chair sliding back on linoleum follows. Light footsteps grow louder and then the door creeks wide open. Dr. Connor is behind the door with a smile as wide as the doorway.

"Goodness, it's been a while. Since November right? And it's February already?"

"Are you sure I'm not interrupting?" I ask.

"Get in here." She grabs my arm with a playful pull and I slip inside.

"From the looks of your desk," I begin, "research is going well." Folders and stapled papers bury her desk.

"Ah, yes," she agrees. "Never a dull moment when publishers are concerned. They loved the *Home Court and Hoops* study and asked for more. A double-edged sword I guess," she says and gestures at the spread.

"That's really cool." I sit in my usual chair. "Congratulations."

"Thanks." She peers over her glasses and raises her eyebrows. "Now I'm assuming you did not come to talk about research?"

"Not directly. You said I could come back when I was ready to talk." I take a deep breath and toy with a pencil on the desk.

Dr. Connor wrinkles her brows and nods her head.

I look down at my feet. "I've been thinking recently about what we've been talking about, the anxiety and everything." I trail off, digging for more courage.

Dr. Connor still sits silently.

"I raise my head resolutely to look at her. "I learned that I'm pretty hard on myself. Not in a good way. Hard on myself in a bad way."

Dr. Connor studies me. "That's quite a confession."

"I feel weird saying it, but it feels true." I recount the incident in Sweden, the uncontrollable tears, and the moment of vulnerability. "It was just too compelling even for me to deny. I couldn't ignore it."

"That must have been quite an experience for you. How are you feeling about it now?"

I consider the question. "For a little while, I found it relieving. But now that it's soaked in more, I guess it means I have to change something. That scares the hell out of me." My insistent tone is apparent to both of us, but Dr. Connor is unshaken by it.

"What do you think you have to change?"

I turn from the window and set the pencil back down on her desk. "I'm not saying that being hard on myself is good. But the discipline and the self-control make me a better athlete. At least I think they do."

"What do you think would happen if you weren't hard on yourself?"

"I don't know. I've always been this way."

She challenges me. "Think about it for a minute. What do you think would happen?"

I close my eyes.

Dr. Connor rises out of her chair and comes to the front of her desk, facing me squarely.

I open my eyes. "I might stop wrestling."

"And if you stopped wrestling, what then?"

"I don't know what I'd do. I wouldn't know what to do. Who would I be?" The truth of it stuns me. I am numb inside.

Dr. Connor puts a hand on my shoulder and sits silently with me for several minutes. "Who were you before you wrestled?"

149

Beneath the Armor of an Athlete

I rise out of my chair and grab a pencil to keep my hands occupied, tossing it back and forth in my hands as I gaze out the window. My hometown of Cedar Falls stares back at me. For a moment I see myself as a young girl, being chased by the neighborhood kids around the backyard. I had clutched a football under my arm and zigzagged around the grass. I had jumped over the dandelions and giggled as I was tackled.

Somehow, between then and now, something changed. The fun of playing sports—of running for the sake of it, of wrestling for the fun of it—had been replaced by fear: the fear of not doing enough, of not being enough, of not being good enough. And with those fears came others: the fear of self-disappointment, the fear of unmet expectations. Before long, I couldn't separate any of it. It was just who I was, how I functioned.

Dr. Connor's question lingers, and I know I owe her an answer. "I guess I was pretty different than I am now."

"If I were going to guess, I'd say that it's pretty hard for you to contain your anxiety when you believe so strongly that wrestling defines you. If you give so much power to that assumption, Lisa, then if you lose the wrestling match, you also lose your identity. That would make me nervous, too."

"Sounds pretty messed up, doesn't it?"

She shakes her head. "I wish someone had suggested the idea to me before I quit basketball. It took me years to figure out that was at the root of my nerves. By then, it was too late."

"So what do I do now?"

She shrugs. "What do you want to do?"

I look out the window. "I guess I have some things to work on. And they don't have much to do with wrestling this time."

"See you in a week to talk about it?" She pushes back her chair to escort me to the door.

"Wait," I start to dig through my bag." I withdraw a white envelope.

"What's this?" She asks.

"Open it and find out."

She looks at me with playful hesitation but finally opens the envelope. She flips to the first of several pieces of paper.

Her eyes flutter left and right as she reads out loud.

"The National Basketball Association Board of Governors is scheduled to approve the concept of the Women's National Basketball Association, the WNBA, in one year."

She looks up from the paper and gasps.

"You were right," I say. "A lot has changed for female basketball players since you were on the court."

"Thank you."

She holds out an open hand before we part, but I hug her instead. I slip away down the hallway as I have done so many times before. I place my lucky stocking cap atop my head and plow into the Iowa winter.

Back in my apartment, I dial the phone number written on the small scratch piece of paper that Steve gave me. Two rings pass, then three, before someone picks up.

"Steve?"

"Speaking."

"It's Lisa. Lisa Whitsett."

"I know which Lisa, silly." He laughs. "Hi."

"Everything going okay in Council Bluffs?"

"Yeah, it's good. I'm here with my mom. She's feeding me every minute of the day it seems. I started student teaching last Monday; I have total hell-raisers for students, of course. I think they gave me everyone they couldn't handle."

"No one better to whip them into shape."

"That's nice of you to say. How's wrestling going?"

I recall the conversation with Dr. Connor. So much has happened since I last spoke to Steve. I feel myself wanting to reach out to him.

"Actually I have a lot to tell you about that, but it's a better conversation in person, I think."

"You think so?"

A long pause lingers. "Are you…seeing anybody? I don't want to disrupt anything—"

"Lisa, come on."

"Well, I just wanted to make sure."

"No. I'm not seeing anyone."

Relief overcomes me. "Then could I see you?"

Another pause hovers. "Are you sure you want to do that?"

"Positive."

"When?"

"Maybe I could come next weekend? Drive up Friday night?"

"You don't mind coming out all this way?" He suggests.

"I have a feeling it will be worth it."

25

November 1994
Phoenix Arizona
Sunkist International Open Tournament

"Sun Devil Arena," I request and I climb into a tattered back seat of the taxicab. A collection of minted air fresheners dangles from the rearview mirror, but still I detect the stench of cigarette smoke. Worn tires squeal as we peel out of the driveway. I look out the dirty back window and the sight of the motel gets smaller, fading into late morning.

The driver deposits me in the parking lot of the arena and I stand alone in the dry Arizona air. I hover briefly until I see a sign over a door that reads Athletes and Coaches Only. A tug on the metal handle reveals a dimly lit annex and corridor. Tumbleweeds of dust roll across my path as the door shuts behind me.

I pause to admire a display case. Silver-plated plaques and wooden trophies boast athletes' records, bronzing the athletes themselves somehow. Framed photographs with autographed signatures and pennant flags decorate the bottom of the case. I raise my hands to the glass and the pane rumbles. I wonder where these athletes are now, how many are still competing, how many have moved on.

Echoes of voices down the hallway entice me to keep moving and I approach the heavy door to the arena. *Focus.* I open the door wide, revealing the magic of the arena. At the top of the stairs, a welcoming burst of warm air sweeps through me. Three amber wrestling mats lay on the ground level. Above each hangs a spotlight with multi-colored gels, digital instruments, and scoreboards. No single sound is discernable amidst wrestlers' grunts and screams. Teenagers run the stairways wildly and expectations of the day whip through my head. I march down the stairs, stepping mindfully around the sticky

153

soda stains and stale kernels of popcorn spectators leave behind.

Scanning the arena for a quiet corner to regain my focus, I catch a glimpse of the main entry. My opponent, the reigning world silver medallist, arrives. I force my eyes away from her and breathe deeply with my eyes closed. *Focus. Focus. Focus.* I adjust my gym bag and cross the arena floor. The rubber soles of my tennis shoes announce my arrival. I approach my opponent with a neutral gaze. I drop my bag loudly two rows behind her.

I zip my warm-up jacket to my chin and pull on my lucky stocking cap in preparation for the first of several warm-up laps around the arena. I glance briefly at the digital clock perched above the arena. Only minutes stand between my opponent and me and the hypnotic pounding of my shoes on the wood floor is a welcomed distraction.

Finally, the announcement thunders over the intercom. "Whitsett, Iowa; LeMark, Illinois; report to mat three. Whitsett and LeMark, mat three." I visit the drinking fountain and gulp a swallow of water. It drains into my stomach and I relish it.

I strip off my blue warm ups and stocking cap in the mat corner, and wear only my singlet and bright yellow wrestling shoes. I stand in the enormous arena and, for a moment, self-consciousness looms. I turn away from the crowds to collect my thoughts, close my eyes and breathe deeply. *Focus. Focus. Focus.* I clap my hands and turn to face my opponent. She is already in the center circle, pacing.

I cross to the middle of the mat and nod a greeting to the referee. I slap the front and back of my legs, my upper arms, and my shoulders. My abdomen contracts and releases in anxious pressure to start. The referee orders us to shake hands, the last civilized gesture spectators will see.

Finally, the whistle blows and we charge each other, jockeying for position and control. I drill my forehead into LeMark's temple and reach inside to her right shoulder. I post my palm, pushing and pulling, hand fighting and grabbing her wrist, hoping for some break in her stance. Finally, she takes an unbalanced step and I drag her to my right side and attack her legs. Our bodies ram into one another and then LeMark abruptly counters again. Neither one of us has control. The referee calls a stalemate, no action, and orders us back to the starting position.

Off the whistle, LeMark shoots a deep double leg attack. I sprawl, throw my hips back, and pound them into her. She struggles beneath me, grunting in recognition of her poor position. I drive bony hips down into her shoulders, forcing pressure on her back. I adjust to a front headlock as tightly as I can, jam my head in her armpit and roll 360 degrees. LeMark emits a frustrated yell as I score the first two points for exposing her back to the mat. I scramble behind her hips for the takedown and one more point. LeMark finds energy stashed away somewhere to keep me from turning her, and the referee brings us back to our feet.

The scoreboard confirms 3-0 in my favor and three minutes left in the match. Off the referee's whistle, I take a deep shot at the same time as my opponent and we collide. My mouth hits her knee; her forehead hits mine. Our collision takes us both out of position. In the scuffle, we jostle to get our hips beneath us again, but at the end of the scramble we are out of bounds. The referee calls us back to the center of the mat.

I sense the time creeping up on me and a glance at the clock confirms it: two minutes remain. Plenty of time for either of us to score and I know I have to get after it. I shoot in to LeMark's left leg. She fights the initial impact but jeopardizes her position. She bangs on the back of my head, but eventually has to give it up or risk more points. I'm ahead 4-0.

I work the top and bottom of my opponent as fifteen seconds click off the clock. I am unable to turn her, and we're put back on our feet with a little more than a minute to go. The whistle blows again and I pound on the back of LeMark's neck to snap her down to the mat. She squirrels out the first time and comes right back in. I pound on her again, my shoulders burning with the slow ache of fatigue. *Focus.* She sets up a single-leg shot and darts to my right leg. I drop my hips and try to roll her through, but I learn that is a mistake. LeMark's hips are in much better position, and suddenly, I am fighting off my back.

She adjusts and feels like 200 pounds against my chest. I bridge to get out, but LeMark lifts my head and clenches her teeth. I bridge again, but LeMark readjusts and wraps around me even tighter. I gasp for a breath, but there is nowhere for my lungs to go. LeMark has my chest completely weighted.

The clock ticks. LeMark grunts as she presses her chest down. I close my eyes and fight, begging that time runs out before she can pin me. My lungs close with the pressure and lack of oxygen. The pain in my chest prompts unbearable thoughts of giving up. *No way.*

The buzzer resonates and LeMark releases to check the score. I lurch off my back, heaving for air. The cloudy spots in front of my eyes slowly diminish as the oxygen returns to my bloodstream. I find my balance and push onto my feet. The referee has awarded LeMark three points for taking me from a standing position to the mat and one point for holding me there for at least five seconds. The score is tied 4 – 4.

The referee jogs to the judges' table shaking his head and I observe a mime of controversy. One official throws controlled gestures, but the two others are shaking their heads. It appears one of the judges believes I was pinned, but the other two disagree.

Meanwhile, my opponent and I await our fate at the center of the mat. LeMark places her hands on her hips, then on her head as she paces in a circle. She scowls and her rib cage heaves. It's nice to know she doesn't feel any better than I do. I turn away to focus and to catch my breath.

Shortly, the referee returns to the center of the mat where LeMark and I circle each other like caged tigers.

"Wrestlers," the referee announces, "we're in sudden death overtime. The clock will be set for two minutes. In that time, the wrestler who scores first wins the match. Understand?"

I nod and wipe the sweat from my eyes. LeMark shakes her head in agreement and still pants. I clap once loudly and assume my stance. The whistle sounds and we're off again, pounding, lurching, and scrambling. Thirty seconds melt away with no score. Worn out, the temptation to get sloppy nips at me. *Focus.*

I coil up and drop step to LeMark's right leg. She pulls it back to counter and I drop to the other side. Her left side is dangerously open and she knows it. She pounds on my head and neck, jams her hips into me, and pummels. I switch my position again, throwing my right arm between widely placed legs and tug on her left arm. Her weight shifts over me and she tumbles to the mat. She scrambles, but it's too late. I pop my head to the outside of her body and recover behind her hips.

I crouch behind her, positioned to turn her if I have to. I fix on the referee hovering over us; everything in the arena seems motionless. The ceiling of stillness shatters as the referee's arm shoots to the sky like a flare. "One!" she shouts to the judges, and the clock sounds in response.

I win in sudden death overtime.

I drop my head to the mat with clasped hands behind my neck. A blissful tear mixes with sweat and slides off my cheek. When I finally push up to my feet, I see LeMark pounding a fist in frustration. The referee grasps my forearm and raises it to the judges. The spectators' encouraging screams, the timing buzzers, and the whistles are muted by my heart, hammering against the inside of my chest, chipping away at the wall of self-doubt.

Spectators have risen to their feet and applaud the over-time effort. The applause still lingers as I wander to the corner of the mat to retrieve my warm-up, reeling in the thrill of it. Some fans make a special trip down to the floor to express congratulations. I accept their words with a thank you and a smile, each time sincerely.

Not long after, the announcement thunders over the sound system: all place-winners in the women's 103-pound weight class should report to the podium. I climb a short set of plat-form stairs and bend down to receive a medal around my neck. I read the inscription on the back, feeling its weight in my humble hands: third place. After the second and first place-winners receive their medals, I wander off the mat toward nowhere in particular, aware of the nothing except the intense joy of the moment.

Hours later, my gym bag is packed full and I march down the stairs through the arena seats, now empty. The lacquered hardwood floors are exposed, except one wrestling mat waiting to be rolled up until it is needed again. It is worn, having been through years of abuse. But it bounces back when I step on it, leaving a shallow depression of my wrestling shoe. I sit on the edge of it and change into street shoes for the plane ride home. *I can't wait to come back.*

I sling my bag over my shoulder and exhale deeply, breathing hope back into the girl who loved wrestling in the first place.

Author Biography

Lisa Whitsett grew up in Cedar Falls, Iowa, where she began the first of twenty-seven years dedicated to sports and athletics. Her experiences as a mental health counselor and her adventures as a business consultant motivated her to write about development, change, and transformation. *Beneath the Armor of an Athlete* was inspired by her own experiences of personal growth as well as her clients'.

Lisa obtained a BA in Sociology from UC San Diego in 1991 and an MA in Mental Health Counseling from the University of Northern Iowa in 1996. Upon graduation, she served the community of Arlington, Texas, as a counselor specializing in career development and also in the treatment of eating disorders.

From 1989-1994, Lisa represented Iowa, California, and the United States in national and international wrestling competition. In 1992, she was named the United States' first female assistant wrestling coach to a male wrestling team in Colorado. Her participation helped lift the ban on females wrestling in that state.

Since retiring from competition, Lisa has remained closely tied to the wrestling community. She serves as a volunteer coach for many teams in Texas and continues to wrestle at camps and clinics. In the summer of 2002, she was a member of the coaching staff for the first Texas Girls' Junior National wrestling team. She plans to remain close to the sport as women's freestyle wrestling has been approved for the 2004 Olympics in Athens, Greece.

Lisa lives Grapevine, Texas, with her husband, Steven Wills. Her twin sister, Laurel, is an actor living in nearby Dallas.

Index

Hornbuckle, Dakota, 124,128, 135
Hornbuckle, Jimi, 123–24, 125, 128, 130–35, 137–38, 138–39, 141, 143–45
Hotel Klippan, 128

Injuries
accident, 52
chronic back pain, 135–36
concussion, 103
Cribiform Plate fracture, 52, 54–57, 72
elbow, 33–34
first wrestling experience after accident, 72
groin pull, 130, 143

Jackson, Tim, 45–46
Junior Nationals, 17

Klippan, Sweden, 128–47
Klippan Cup, 142

Lannum, Chris, 88, 89, 90–94
Las Vegas, Nevada, 1–5, 101–4
1991 National Freestyle Wrestling Tournament, 1–5
1992 National Freestyle Wrestling Tournament, 101–4
Las Vegas Convention Center, 1
LeMark Jennifer (opponent), 154–7

Meningitis, 57, 60

National Basketball Association Board of Governors, 151
National Freestyle Wrestling Tournament (Las Vegas)
1991 tournament, 1–5
1992 tournament, 101–4
NCAA wrestling championship, 38
Newspaper reporter (unidentified), 29–31, 34

Oklahoma State University, 24, 38
Oliver, Roye, 117–18, 124, 125, 127, 136–37, 139
Olympics, 41

Phoenix, Arizona, 109–13, 123–27, 153–58
Sunkist International Open Tournament, 109–13, 124, 153–58
training camp, 123–27
Pierce Dan, 67–68, 70–71, 78, 80, 86–87, 88, 90, 96
Prado, Marie, 124–25, 129
Progressive relaxation, 37, 43, 108

Roderick, Myron, 38–39, 42, 43
Roshanzamir, Afsoon, 124

Saunders, Tricia, 3–4, 125, 142
Smith, John, 41–43, 45

State High School Wrestling tournament (Denver, 1992), 88–94
Steve (boyfriend). *See* Wills, Steven
Sudden death overtime, 156
Sun Devil Arena, 153
Sunkist International Open Tournament (Phoenix)
1992 tournament, 109–13, 124
1994 tournament, 153–58
Sunkist Kids wrestling club, 24
Sway, Mister (father of Nick and Troy), 32–33, 76, 89–90, 91, 94
Sway, Nick, 27, 32–33, 65, 71, 74–77, 88
Sway, Troy, 27, 65, 76, 77–78, 88, 89–90, 91, 92–93, 94
Sweden. *See* Klippan, Sweden

Tournament matches
Lisa's, 3–4, 66, 103, 111–13, 140–41, 154–57
other wrestlers, 17, 90–92, 94, 141–42
Training regimen, 138
cooling down, 26–27
drilling, 29, 135
interval training, 107
Plyometric work, 107–8, 114
pushups, 45–46
run/jogging/sprint 25–27, 31, 102–3, 107, 126–27, 130, 134